ISBN: 978-0-578-51567-0 (Paperback)

The events and conversations in this book have been set down to the best of the author's ability, though some names and details have been changed or removed to protect the privacy of the individuals involved and to provide cohesiveness to the narrative.

Front cover design by: Youness El Hindami

Illustrations by: Charity Rissler

First printing edition 2019

www.ThisArtistsLife.com

Where the Willow Weeps

Charity Rissler

Table of Contents

Author's Note

I would like to say this is a true story—which it is, apart from names being changed, but a more accurate description is that it is a true memory, and a true memory is not the same as a true and accurate account of history. As I write this, most of the events in this book took place several years ago. It is also hard because the purpose of this story is to tell what the Lord has done for me in my life. This is my testimony, but naturally, other people's stories interact with my story. I will try and render an accurate account to the best of my ability, but I am only human, and I know there will be inaccuracies in the tale. The core pieces in the story, though some details (dates, names, particular words spoken) may be off, the layout of the story is true as I perceived it.

I also would like to say that I hold no malice for anyone in The Message. Some of my dearest friends and family grew up in it, and some of them are still a part of it—whether they are fully immersed, trying to leave, or have left. I know that the way I was treated when I left was the way I would have treated those who left while I was in it. That being said, I feel that for the most part, those in The Message have a strong conviction that it is true, and if you think something is true, it shows that your actions should follow suit. How can I feel hatred for a person who is doing what they believe is true? No, all I can do for such a person is pray for them.

Again, the purpose of this story is to show my testimony of how the Lord Jesus rocked the world I thought was true, and showed me a different path, a path filled with His grace and mercy. A path that, through His unshaken love, made all the accounts in this story—that appear on the surface broken and skewed—to be perfectly worked out for good that I can glorify Him; so that all who read my story can likewise glorify Him. For God is good.

1

Background

Hello, my name is Charity Rissler. Let me tell you a little about myself. I'm a Christian, an artist, a writer—to name a few of the things I am. I have many things, some of which included a pretty, blue, rustic-looking rug, more art supplies than I know what to do with, a glossy record player that plays jazz, and an old Toyota Corolla—*conveniently* the color of duct tape.

Other things of value I own? As many do, I have my memories, and as I share my faith, talents, space, jazz records, and car with people...so too, I share this with you.

With trembling hands, I begin a story I so far remove myself from that I wonder if it really happened. The word "cult" is just a word. Yet, to me, that word is a story, my story—a story filled with moments that make me wonder at this world. That makes me want to listen to jazz—a piece of music that was once not allowed for me, and thank God that the world isn't what I imagined it was when I was a child and a young teenager.

My story of being in a cult begins with a man who was dead long before I was born. The founder and focal point of The Message was William Branham who lived from 1909 (though the date of his birth is speculated)[1] and died in 1965. He was born in Kentucky, the oldest of ten children. He claimed that at his birth, a Light came whirling through the window, about the size of a pillow, circled where he was, and went down on the bed.[2] William Branham also said that he had mystical experiences from an early age; he was trained as a Baptist preacher, but eventually, had Pentecostal leanings in his teachings. Branham claimed to have received an angelic visitation on a mountain top in Arizona where he opened the seals, commissioning his healing ministry and launching his campaigning career in mid-1946[3]. His fame spread rapidly as crowds were drawn to his stories of angelic visitations and reports of miracles happening at his meetings. Although today, his work is mostly forgotten, he left a lasting impact on the charismatic movement. At the time, his interdenominational meetings were the largest religious meetings ever held in some American cities. His ministry impacted and initiated many emulators and set in motion the broader healing revival that later became the modern Charismatic movement. From 1955, William Branham's campaigning and popularity began to decline as the Pentecostal churches began to withdraw their support from the healing campaigns for primarily financial reasons. By 1960, William Branham transitioned into a teaching ministry.

Even though William Branham has been long gone, his followers estimated to be between half a million and a million worldwide.[4] Despite the digitalization and transcription of his taped sermons, as well as documented evidence that would disprove him being who he said he was (a prophet), The Message continues to spread.

Any facts that would paint his doctrine or character in a less than perfect light are irrelevant to Message believers because they don't see anything that contradicts The Message—I was once blind to those points as well. The thought that anything contrary could be true is so foreign, that it would seem absurd to think it anything but a fantasy. Sure, if you share your faith with friends outside of the group, they might pay attention and intervene with you, asking you hard, real questions. The magic of such a group; however, that makes it so compelling, is that those friends are discouraged. The family that doesn't believe should be prayed over, but in general, anyone not thinking the same as you are not to be reasoned with, and we were taught you shouldn't waste your time with them. Even if we had close friends outside of The Message, we would be scared to share our faith with them.

I remember being told many things to discourage from sharing. Firstly, you were going to heaven, and most of the people around you weren't, so any friendship you formed was doomed from the beginning. Therefore, the likelihood of feeling like you could be that vulnerable to share what you believed with a non-believer was very slim. We were also predisposed to assume that they would reject the message we told them (and we wouldn't have been wrong), and if they rejected it with negative words, then we would be judged for that. So, we were told that if we shared it, we would have to be doubly cautious, lest they speak ill of The Message and we bear the brunt of their words in judgment.

Also, we were told that we were better than them, in so many words they (those in ministry) combed our egos. We would judge the world; even other Christians would be at our mercy come judgment time. God had hand-selected us, and we were left to assume that for whatever reason, He hadn't handpicked the rest of the world. They were inferior, blind to the divine revelation we had been given. The world was ending, and it was too late for them. Unless God opened their eyes, there was no effort we could use to entice them to see our beliefs in any light other than radical. We didn't deny the beliefs as being radical. In fact, that was part of the charm. The difference—we thought—between our beliefs and other radical beliefs, is that ours were true.

Miracles vindicated our beliefs, mind you, not ones I'd seen, but I knew people who'd seen miracles, or at least in hindsight, I knew people who knew people who'd seen miracles. If you asked me if I'd seen miracles, I would have said yes. I've seen a lot of unexplainable things, but when I stop, and on a case by case basis, go through the events, I do see how I was primed to see miracles. The same way that my optimism in my daily life now primes me to see people doing good things, and I see great opportunities for me and others because I assume they are there. Because I believe God is a good God and answers prayer, I see those answers to prayer all around me. I'm looking for the good, so even in a subjectively 'bad' situation, I can't help but notice the possible good in the situation.

It was the same when I was in The Message; I saw what I believed was there and was looking for. I always heard stories of miracles of days gone by and recent miracles. So, I 'saw' them, in the chaos of a cult, I saw a beautiful mirage I knew to be true. I saw miracles, smiling faces, divine wisdom, and insight laid upon us by the voice of—we thought—God Himself, who counted us worthy to receive this doomsday message. He was capable of anything, and we were likewise capable of anything because God was on our side.

The specific cult I followed was—I guess you could call it—a cult within a cult. While William Branham may have taken the Bible out of context and imposed his own impression of the doctrine, so Brother Coleman did the same with Brother Branham's message. Yes, you will sometimes see me refer to people as 'brother' and 'sister' as that is how I referred to them growing up. It was both a familial greeting for people in The Message and a title of respect. William Branham talked about seven church ages. Brother Coleman's claim to fame was when he linked up the seven church ages with the seven thunders mentioned in Revelation 10:3-4, going still farther, to place us on a timeline that said we were living in the echo of that final trumpet sound, which would mean the world was ending.

You could recognize a woman in The Message; the rules for us were hair uncut, skirts below the knee, necklines not lower than two fingers below the collarbone (Though some families including mine were cautious about showing even that), no underarm showing, no form-fitting skirts, no slits (even if the skirt was longer, and the slit didn't go above the knee), no sleeveless tops or dresses, we couldn't wear swimsuits. Some people made exceptions to this rule when on vacation, but my parents hesitated to allow even that unless it was an all-girl situation. We couldn't have earrings or tattoos, couldn't wear makeup or wear bold nail colors.

For church specifically, we were required not to wear any denim (Though denim skirts were a staple outside of church), and we had to wear shoes (not flip-flops or other open-back shoes), stockings, and no hat. For church, specifically, men had to dress up and not wear a hat.

The general dress code for men wasn't as strict, depending on the church you were in, shorts might have been a no-go, and they couldn't take their shirt off in the presence of a lady who wasn't their wife, and they had to keep their hair nicely cut with no beard. Then, of course, no tattoos or piercings, no jewelry, and probably assumed, but no makeup either.

I remember one particular day after church a meeting was held for the ladies, telling us that we needed to wear slips in church to make sure that there wasn't any sheerness to the dresses or skirts we would wear. We were told that because men were wired differently, we would cause them to sin if we wore something too provocative. May heaven forgive us if we dared wear something like a push-up bra underneath all that modest attire and ruin the whole thing. If a man stumbled into and entertained lust for one of us, we would be held accountable at the judgment.

Brother Coleman's church was split up into little groups of around 150 people—consequently, the textbook number for optimum group collaboration.[5] There was a church in New York where Brother Coleman lived, one in Pennsylvania which was considered 'one' with the New York church, and to be respected as highly. Pennsylvania was my home church. There was also a church in England, one in Tucson Arizona, another in Belgium, Trinidad, Puerto Rico, and France. There may have been a few others that slip my memory right now. There were also individuals around the world and small house churches that streamed the services weekly. People in every state, and Canada, China, Congo, Nigeria, Czech, Latvia...to name a few.

New York and Pennsylvania held a certain kind of seniority, such that I, being born there, vs. in another one of the many churches, gave me a certain built-in privilege. I knew that when I was older, I would have no lack of suitors, assuming that I would not be particularly bad looking. That is because people of other countries were eager to marry into

America, especially New York or Pennsylvania, at the heart of where the end time messages would be preached. No matter where we lived we believed simultaneously that the world would end before we grew up, but also, that perchance it didn't, we would marry into The Message and choose our location and vocation depending on whether or not there was a church close enough to commute to every Sunday, at least.

2

The Predestined Child

And we know that for those who love God all things work

together for good, for those who are called according to his

purpose.

Romans 8:28 (ESV)

I knocked on the bathroom door again after several tiresome trials. This time, the voice that answered was different—yet again. "Hey, it was my turn to get in there next; I've been waiting longer than you!"

"You weren't ready." I was, in fact, 'ready,' but that word really meant stay outside the bathroom door with all the things you could possibly need to be carried with you, not abandoning your post for a moment lest another take the opportunity.

I wasn't particularly bothered; after all, from a young age, I knew the routine. I had twelve siblings crammed into a huge Victorian house with a whopping 2 and ½ baths. One of those bathrooms had an actual claw-footed bath with peeling white paint, leftover from one of the previous owners at some point in the past 160 or so years. Sometimes, it was fewer bathrooms because one or two of the toilets got backed up. As it was, there was always only one stand-up shower, which in the mornings was coveted. Especially Sunday mornings, when it was in almost constant use from 6 AM to the time we scurried out to church around 8AM. The bathtub was a poor substitute for desperate persons who hadn't thought to get up earlier or shower the night before.

Eventually, we'd file into our fifteen-passenger van which was the perfect size to accommodate everyone, the older more respected siblings would be in their preferred seats by the window or close to the front, and the younger ones left to scramble for the next best. Whenever per chance we had a guest, or upon the rarer chance that a love interest of one of my older siblings was along, the smallest among us would share a seatbelt so that an extra car wouldn't be needed on the 45-minute drive to church.

You'd think it would be weird. The 12 siblings, the homeschooling (which I've yet to mention), or the mansion with a tower and massive stone basement that would scare the living daylights out of you every time you went to look for your clean laundry in the middle of rural Pennsylvania. I think some part of me knew at a young age that there was something very unusual about the whole setup, but it was a way of life for me. Not only that but there are aspects of it I really enjoyed. Homeschooling, for instance, isn't something that is for everyone, but it did me good. It taught me self-discipline, work ethic, and gave me time to prioritize my art (visual and writing) over other subjects. The big family taught me social skills despite being homeschooled—not to mention the fact that I count my family members as dear friends. Well, that's enough ruminating—back to the story we go.

We tried to be at church by 9 AM, but our big van normally pulled into that crowded parking lot closer to 10. At some point, somebody would frantically point out that my hair wasn't done, and it might have been quickly tied up in the kitchen at breakfast, or in the car, or if I had tried to get a seat in the car early, and it wasn't noticed in the scurrying, then right before I went into church, my mom or one of my older sisters would fix it as the others went on before me. On this morning, that was the case.

I remember how much I dreaded having my hair done; it was very long, and I was very energetic. My hair often wound up matted behind my neck, which made detangling it a pain. Not to mention that the times when I couldn't avoid my hair getting done would be when we were going out. Such times were usually a chaotic scramble, which meant that the infamous mat had to be detangled, and it had to be detangled *fast*. My mom took this opportunity to ask me if I'd done my memory verse for Sunday school. I hadn't. My weekly memory verse would be practiced for a little on the car ride home from church (soon after it was assigned). Usually, I would forget to study it mid-week; so it was drilled into my head on the car ride to Sunday School because my siblings and I never skipped the memory verse. I pulled the verse out of my little plastic blue binder and went over it repeatedly, in-between squeals of discomfort and tears at the terror that was getting my hair into an orderly state. The terror ended, however, and my mom would put the brush back in her overflowing bag that was five times bigger than my head, and we'd hurry inside.

On the way inside, I felt my hair to try and visualize whether all that pain was worth it, and I brushed my hand over the tight high bun where my mom had somehow tied up all of my couple feet of hair in a tiny little combed knot. When I lifted my arms to check the state of my hair however, my mom noticed some of my underarms were visible, so we stopped at the bathroom before service so she could try to fish a pair of safety pins out of her purse to make a fix to my wardrobe malfunction.

In-between 9 AM and 10 AM was time to pray, while 10 AM to 11 PM was song service, during which time the offering was passed around and the children would exit the sanctuary and join Sunday School as adults stayed for service. I didn't even get a chance to sit down because we stood for a song service, and it was long. I counted it prudent that my mother had safety-pinned my sleeves because people raised their hands a lot during worship, and Risslers shouldn't be caught with their armpits showing. It was pretty late already, so I didn't have to wait long to exit to Sunday School where partitions had been set up in the lobby.

As I walked in, I saw that my friend, Lily, was already there, so I eagerly sat next to her. She didn't come to the Wednesday night service, so I only saw her once a week. She leaned over and asked me what the verse was; she hadn't been there the week before. She whispered back what I said over and over again, but thankfully, the teacher called my name first.

"Now faith is the substance of things hoped for and the evidence of things not seen."

"And where is it found?" Sister Debby asked me.

"Oh, easy, Hebrews 11:1."

Sister Debby offered praise and put a sticker next to my name. We got a sticker for attendance, another for homework completed, and another for memory verse. The Risslers were always at the top because we attended every service and made sure to do all the assigned homework and scripture memory. Whenever we got five stickers, we'd get to pick from the treasure chest. I proudly turned in my homework, which I'd gotten done in the car on the way.

Lily was next. Her freckles beaded nervously. She'd forgotten, but how could she? I had literally just heard her say the whole thing.

"No, you know it," I insisted.

"Do you want to try?" Sister Debby asked. I mouthed the first couple words, and at the teacher's added prompting, Sister Debby reluctantly gave her the sticker.

Homework was handed out at snack, so I seized the opportunity to finish it. As a nine-year-old, I had only recently got comfortable with reading. It was a coloring page, with a couple of questions to answer. But now, I was taking advantage of my newfound independence since I no longer had to ask for help to start my homework.

The homework was something about new beginnings and a picture of a sunrise.

"Charity, you get to pick from the treasure chest," Sister Debby announced at the end. This was my favorite thing; my parents rarely bought us new things; they were frugal in the way they spent their money, so most of my toys were hand-me-downs. In other words, to have a choice in what I got gave me a thrill. There was a little mini doll who had cute yarn hair with bangs in the front. I shuttered. Bangs meant that she had had a haircut, which was wrong, but that was the only new thing in the box since last I saw it a couple of weeks prior. Ruth, my second cousin and best friend, looked over my shoulder and sighed as another kid took the last cat plush. I reluctantly chose the doll with bangs. I promised I'd meet Lily and Ruth after the service at the tree, and thanked Sister Debby on my way out of the room. Sister Debby stopped me as she saw my half-finished coloring page.

"Why is the sky purple?" she asked.

"Sometimes, in the sunrise, there is a little bit of purple."

She contorted her eyebrows and snorted, "No, there isn't. Sunrises are red, yellow, and orange."

"Yes…I know, but sometimes, there's purple in them."

"No…," she leaned down to my level. "Charity, there is no purple in a sunrise."

"Yeah, there is; I've seen it."

She laughed again, but then soberly conclude, "No, there isn't."

"Well, I see purple in sunrises sometimes…" I said, in some kind of mumble if not loud. Although she didn't reply, so maybe it was only in my head.

I would always linger as long as I could after Sunday School because I knew I'd have to sit still in church and I didn't have a clue what was being talked about. I would get some water at the water fountain, take a bathroom break, and try to time it right so I wouldn't get a suspicious look from Brother Rece, who seemed always to be able to read my rebellious mind with but a glance.

Service was rarely live; if it were, I wouldn't get away with a coloring book or drawing, or any other form of entertainment because if it were live, the adults would be jumping from their seated position and saying amen, something I was supposed to do too. After all, I was almost 10 years of age. This time, however, it was a video recording of our pastor; Brother Coleman. He was in his late 70s and couldn't make it to church. I wondered to myself if I had ever actually seen him in person. He was always so sick he couldn't make it to church, but he was really smart and knew a lot. He must have been brilliant because I couldn't understand him. I took hope, however, that when I was older, I would understand him, and by then, he would be better. I knew this because everyone prayed for him and said he'd be better. He'd be preaching live again, and that hope is what I ended every prayer with every morning, every night, and before every meal "...and heal Brother Coleman; amen."

The video was from his office, and he sat in a kingly brown leather chair; his balding black hair combed neatly, and he wore a black suit and purple tie. It was recorded recently, but his voice was tired, not provoking shouts of amen from the people as per usual. I saw the glow in people's eyes as they soberly watched the screen and nodded. He must be a really great man, I mused to myself. I reached into my mom's bag looking for paper, but there was none—only coloring books— always coloring books.

So, I colored, but as I looked at the purple crayon, I changed my mind; I'd prefer to draw. So, I made use of the inside covers of the coloring books and any pages in the books that had a lot of empty space. I would tell a story in my mind which drowned out the noise of Brother Coleman's voice, a narrative and illustrations complex enough to last until 1 or 3 PM, whenever the service let out. I knew that I wouldn't always be able to draw in church because that wasn't something the big kids out of Sunday School did, but there were still a couple of years between now and then, so I wasn't worried. Surely, I would be able to understand by then, and listening to the full duration of teaching wouldn't be an issue.

My tummy was rumbling when service finally let out, but I ignored it and hurried out to meet my friends at the tree.

It was a huge weeping willow; whose branches were kept trimmed by the eager little hands that reached up to grab them. It also was the base in any game of freeze tag. Eventually, my friends' parents would collect them, usually before my parents came for me.

Today though, Ruth was still here, so we played together. Ruth had something in her parent's car that she wanted to show me, so we headed that way. She had a little card for me with a cat drawing on it. Ruth was obsessed with cats, so I liked them too. Ruth had paper, so I asked to borrow some, and we both scribbled out pictures together in silence, Ruth was the one to break it. "Charity! The van!" I scrambled to push aside my papers and hopped out of Ruth's car and sprinted, but I was too far away to attract the attention of my family driving away. Frank and Miriam were walking towards us, and seeing my distress, they turned and saw the van disappear.

"We can call them," Miriam said sweetly, letting go of Frank's hand, "…oh, I only have their landline; Frank, do you have their number?"

Frank turned to me, "Charity, what's one of your parent's numbers?" I started to answer, and Frank began to dial but as I got six digits in, I realized there were half a dozen number sequences that popped in my head next, and I couldn't tell which ones my brain was spewing out and which one was actually right, if any.

I rubbed my eyes and let out a sob. Miriam hugged me, "I'm sure they'll call us soon, and if so, we can meet them, or we'll call them when they arrive at home. For now, you can come back with us and borrow Ruth's clothes."

This new idea was very agreeable to me, and all my tears instantly dried. I loved going to Ruth's house, though it didn't happen too often because Ruth's house was ten minutes on the other side of the church, which meant almost two hours of driving for one of our parents to drop the other off. I was excited.

I headed inside, and Miriam said something about how messy it was. I laughed, "You should see our place."

In hindsight, I know that Miriam had seen my place, and to answer that statement with anything other than "well, let me just get the table cleared off," would have given me verbal proof from an adult to report back to my mother in hopes that our house would be cleaner. Also, in hindsight, however, I did grow up in a family of 15, including my parents, and for me to say that my house could have been perfectly clean growing up, would make my mother a superhero and this book fiction, which it's not.

Soon enough, Ruth and I were helping to set the table, David, Ruth's older brother, who was my age, may have helped or been playing with Legos. As we began to eat, the phone rang, and I heard my mother's panicked squeals come through the phone.

"Yes, I thought you might be home soon; we were going to call your landline. I don't have your cell saved, and Charity couldn't remember—oh yes, yes, she's here."

Miriam paused, and even without the speaker, I could make out my mom verbal processing how on earth she could forget one of her children at church and how SURE she had been that she had done a headcount.

"What do you want to do?" Miriam asked, "it's already getting late, do you want to come and get her? Or she could borrow Ruth's clothes and spend the night?" My mom sighed

31

and said more things I couldn't make out. Ruth was watching her mother, clasping her hands together and using pleading eyes with her mother.

"Let's just do that then; no, I don't mind. We can figure it out tomorrow. Don't worry about it; we love having Charity; she's always so helpful. It's really fine." Ruth and I both began doing happy dances, and David yawned unenthusiastically.

So excited that I was to stay the night and starving since it was passed three and none of us had eaten since breakfast; we ate merrily together, spurred on by Frank's jokes. Then we helped clear the table, played a board game, and went off to bed. The next day came, and Ruth asked if another friend of hers—a neighbor down the road—could come over too, and so she did. That is what I loved about summer; my friends were free. As for me, I had homeschooling all year round, though it was pretty lax in the summer; I could always rearrange my schedule, as it would be rearranged anyway depending on what my family had going on.

Jenny got there, Ruth had told me about Jenny, even referred to her as her best friend, a concept so foreign to me. After thinking about it, I had concluded that if I had a best friend, it was probably Ruth, and if it was Ruth, how could she have another best friend? It left me completely befuddled. There she was though, Jenny herself, and she was wearing pants.

Now dear reader, I suppose you don't know the significance of Ruth's friend wearing pants. I did have a neighbor friend too who had pants; at least, I had had her as a friend, but she didn't come over much anymore. We would always jump on the trampoline, but her mother had told her she couldn't come anymore because she had told her mom that when we jumped on the trampoline together, she sometimes saw our underwear—which rightly enough made the mother a little uneasy. Fair enough, but at this moment in time, Ruth had a friend with pants and not only was she a friend with pants, but she was Ruth's best friend. I looked her up and down, her pretty red hair in *bangs*. How could she be Ruth's friend? She wasn't like us at all.

However, once I got to play with her, I quickly forgot my envy and that this girl was different than us. She liked to play games too; she liked to read and tell stories, and she could also draw fun cartoons of cats. It occurred to me that she was another fun girl like us, somebody I could also be friends with. All good things end, however, sometimes right when we realize they are good, and we said goodbye to Jenny. Then when Frank got home from work, we all, including David, so he could play with my younger brothers, headed over to the mansion for dinner, and to drop me off. It had been such a good Monday, and I was sad to be home.

I changed my tune a little when I got inside those big doors and saw how the house shined and smelled of cleaning supplies. Ruth lingered outside and chased one of the stray cats. Dinner was being made, and it smelled so good. Peter saw me and grumbled, "You're so lucky. You got to be at Ruth's and we had to clean up."

"I was left there..." I reminded him, unconvinced as I said it that it was actually a bad thing. Peter didn't seem to be convinced either. "Is David here?" Peter asked, and I nodded, so he forgot his trial, walked past me, and went to find his friend. Ruth was soon in, sulking that the cats didn't want her love. Miriam and Frank came after, Miriam holding a pan of brownies. My mom went to greet her, her hair still dripping from the shower.

"Thank you so much!" She almost collapsed onto Miriam, but realizing her hair was still in need of drying; she cut the hug short. "I really appreciate you taking care of Charity. That's crazy that happened; I counted everyone, and we didn't see her outside the car. I think we would have seen her."

"I was in their car," I said, as though that explained the whole reason I was left behind.

"It wasn't a problem at all; we had so much fun, and Charity is always such a help. Thank you for inviting us to dinner, I brought brownies," Miriam extended her arms, "where should I put these?"

"Hope, can you?" Hope broke the glare she had been giving me and took the pan from Miriam.

"Thank you; you didn't have to and thank you for driving so far."

"It really isn't a problem," sweet Miriam insisted yet again.

"I'm sorry I'm such a mess, let me go and dry my hair, and I'll be back." So, my mom hugged me and retreated upstairs, leaving my dad to fill in where she left off.

I went upstairs without Ruth, as she had dashed outside with renewed energy, thinking she would try coaxing one of the cats to her yet again. I promised to meet her outside, but I needed to change out of her clothes into mine. I went upstairs with all my things, and I remembered the doll I'd gotten from Sunday School. My parents wouldn't approve of the bangs, so I took scissors and cut them close to where they were attached to the head. Hope, who I shared my room with, walked in right at the end. "You cut her hair!" she gasped in disbelief as she snatched the doll from me.

"So it looks more natural, now it doesn't look like it was cut!" Hope spun out of the room and around the corner, doll in hand, to show my mother who was drying her hair with a towel in the bathroom.

I ran after to try and explain myself. Before I could, Hope was rambling, "Mom! Look!" I couldn't tell if Hope was tattle-telling on me or if she was telling on me so that my mother could explain the confusing act. Cutting the doll's hair could be a sign I fantasized cutting mine, and if that were the case, it would have been considered a grave breach in my character. Another sister was walking by and heard the commotion.

"What?" She took the doll in her own hands and gasped in disbelief. My heart was pounding as I opened my mouth yet again to try and make them understand.

"It LOOKED like she had cut hair and I didn't want it to look like she had cut hair!" I realized no one heard what I said, for they seemed instead to be examining the doll in some state of shock.

My mom turned to me, her face full of disappointment and said quietly, "Charity, why would you do this? Why would you cut her hair?"

I opened my mouth a final time, my heart pounding, wondering if I had actually stated the words I thought I had, and trying to say them yet again but all I could muster was a tearful, "I-I-I don't know why."

3

The Rise of a Charlatan

*Beware of false prophets, who come to you in sheep's clothing
but inwardly are ravenous wolves. You will recognize them by
their fruits. Are grapes gathered from thornbushes, or figs from
thistles? So, every healthy tree bears good fruit, but the
diseased tree bears bad fruit. A healthy tree cannot bear bad
fruit, nor can a diseased tree bear good fruit. Every tree that
does not bear good fruit is cut down and thrown into the fire.
Thus you will recognize them by their fruits.*

Matthew 7:15-20 (ESV)

My childhood faded slowly into adulthood; by the time
I turned 12, I was adjusting to sitting up front at church with
my sister Hope, outside of Sunday school. I was ready and
willing, although I didn't always understand what was being

preached, I began to realize that wasn't the point. In fact, if you could understand things perfectly, then there would be no mystery. If you could understand things perfectly, then anyone could preach. I realized it wasn't so much your level of understanding of what was being preached but your attitude towards what was being taught. It was something bigger than 'merely presenting scripture' to help you understand life and God—this was a mystery unfolding before our eyes, a mystery to us, a chosen people, that we couldn't understand, but one day, we would.

There was a certain energy in church that compelled me to stand to my feet and say amen with everyone else. I couldn't explain it, other than at the time, I would have referred to it as the 'anointing' or the 'fire'. The air was always thick with expectancy like someone had left the gas on, and people were playing with matches. It felt intoxicating, and we thought every Sunday service only brought us closer to something big. Was it the second coming of Christ? Was it Brother Coleman's healing? Was it something else? I was old enough to take communion and I couldn't go to Sunday School anymore, and I didn't have to sit with my parents anymore during the services. I could sit in the third or fourth row with my friends or other single/widowed women, while the front two rows were reserved for the men, and the families sat in the back.

I remember something new was happening in church. I mean there was always a new message or teaching, but this was a new something. I remember a couple of times there were words "directly from God" that a man had "seen on the wall," were read from the pulpit. In biblical times, handwriting on the wall was something that Daniel saw and read to Belshazzar, King of Babylon. In that illustration found in Daniel 5, it was a sign of the end times. Was it now the end time? What was going on? First, it was read once, and then there was another, and to my and others' great excitement, the messages poured in almost every Sunday. My family and other core families in the church were no longer the only ones eager not to miss a sermon. Even Wednesday nights started filling up because no one wanted to miss words from God.

What were the first writings? I can hardly remember now; except I remember each word hitting me very personally. It was—we all thought—words directly from God to us, *live*. The summer convention was coming up in July. It was the same time every year, but this year felt different. This convention was different because we had words from God. Not only that, but Jason Baker would be there—the man who had the gift to see the words of God on the wall—he would speak at the convention! I don't remember when the obscure man made his first appearance at the pulpit. I think he was called up once to give his testimony, and he started preaching too. Who knew he would also have the gift of evangelism? He prophesied that Brother Coleman would be healed at the convention and would preach. We were all praying that would be the case, and as it drew closer, our excitement peaked.

Our van pulled up to the huge convention center the first day. I had my long hair loose to my knees, which I was very proud of, but between my hair acting like a long scarf, long skirts with pantyhose and short sleeves, and the long car ride in our old van whose air conditioning was questionable, the hot July sun was felt especially keenly. You would imagine that because there were two services instead of one, that the convention services would lean on the short side, but that was generally not the case, in fact, this summer especially, it was quite the opposite. A couple of years prior, I had fainted in the line at the 'Old Country Buffet' of exhaustion, hunger, and dehydration. I remember the one egg I had early that morning before going to the convention center did very little for me by 3 PM in the 90-degree heat.

This year, however, I was older, and even though the services were long, my stomach growled, and my head hurt, I would zoom right past the water fountain and back into service, for fear of missing a word that was said. Jason didn't preach the first service. I remember looking behind me and seeing a girl my height with brown hair in a braid, who held a solemn countenance. I'd never seen her before in my life, but I felt drawn to her. The way she braided her hair was the way I usually braided mine. I felt like I wanted to say hi, but couldn't bring up the nerve.

The first service ended, and I saw Lily. She hadn't been around much, and I ran to her; she was talking to someone, "Are you a Rissler?" the person asked her, "you look like one of the Risslers."

"No, I'm not..." She seemed happy that I rescued her from the stranger's question, and I was eager to embrace her. Apparently, brown hair and brown eyes made that question flow freely from people's tongues and invited hugs from strangers. I embraced Lily and said I missed her while the stranger went away, and I asked her where she had been. "I don't really know, I've been busy with a lot of things. My dad makes me do horse shows; we've been going to a lot of those..."

It was then it happened; as Lily was releasing me from that hug and answering my question that I felt a little tug on my hair. All at once, I felt a sharp pain, and confused; I shot out of her arms, realizing in the same moment that my hair was caught, caught on a moving person and that moving person was an oblivious man walking into the crowd. Trying not to draw TOO much attention to myself, I tried to get HIS attention, following him closely until I finally placed my hand on him and said, "Brother, excuse me." He turned around and leaned down to meet my gaze.

"Are you all right?" he asked in a crystal-clear British accent. I held back tears and explained as I reached out awkwardly.

"My hair…"

"Yes, what about your hair?"

"It's…it's caught on your button…" I fumbled.

"Oh," he awkwardly fiddled with it, and as soon as it was free, I pulled away to find Lily again, but she was nowhere in sight.

Soon, my sister, Hope, caught my hand, "Charity, this is Aphia! The one I told you about; she's going to stay with our family this summer."

I smiled broadly; it was the girl with the braid, "I saw you in church!"

She smiled back too, "It is nice to meet you; I saw you too." Her French accent made me giddy; I'd never heard a French accent before; this was my first one-on-one experience.

"How old are you?" I asked.

"I'm good, and you?" she eagerly responded, but Hope corrected her, speaking slowly.

"She asked how old you are?" Aphia quickly corrected herself and told me she was 11.

"Oh! Then you can go to the kids' thing; it should be starting soon. They have lunch, or at least, they did last year."

Aphia looked at Hope at a loss, "Oh, it's an activity for kids who are 8 to 12. Charity and I are too old, but you can go." Hope's pace made her understand.

"Oh, yes, I heard about that; I think my dad signed me up. I will go." We spent a little more time getting acquainted with Aphia before helping her find the room the kids would be in.

The next day, we saw her again, and after the first service, I asked her if the kids' activity was fun, and she nodded in the affirmative. Lily and some other friends were going in a parent's car to a restaurant nearby for lunch, and as this fact was made known to Aphia, she exclaimed her desire to go with us.

"Don't you want to go to the kids' thing again? You said it was fun?"

Aphia sighed, "No, I didn't understand the question. I want to go with you."

The next night, Brother Edwards preached; a tall British man with silver hair and a charming personality, sat next to Jason Baker, my favorite pastor. A couple more days and Brother Coleman would be healed. After my whole short life waiting, I thought I would finally shake Brother Coleman's hand.

I paused as I recall the bizarre events of 2011. There were prophecies and power plays, strange doctrines that said things like Michael the archangel was really Jesus, that Brother

Coleman was perfect, that the seven thunders were seven birth pains that would birth us into perfection as well. Jason would call people out from the audience, speak healing, or discernment into their life as I had heard William Branham had once done. Jason prophesied that on July 7th Brother Coleman would be healed and walk in the sanctuary with a new body of a 21-year-old man. He would preach a final service, and the rapture would take place. Maybe it was just the isolation, but in that moment, everything felt very normal. These were my people; they understood me like nobody else would. Together, we were a part of something huge, and besides, we believed that other people weren't going to heaven, even 'regular' Christians. Or at least, they weren't going in the rapture and would be tormented in the tribulation period discussed in Revelation 7:14.

On July 6th was Jason Baker's turn to preach yet again. The sermon was on repentance; specifically, that Brother Coleman hadn't been healed yet, because God was waiting for the people to turn to their brother and make things right.

Brother Coleman's healing might be the forthcoming of the rapture, and all things needed to be made right. We needed to be filled with the experience of the Holy Spirit, and we also needed to be perfected in brotherly love. So, in this particular sermon, he told us that we needed to repent. We had to seek out that person who we hold a grudge against and make it right. Go outside and call them if you had to, or move from your seat and find them in the crowd because if you didn't make things right, Brother Coleman would not be healed the following day as the prophecy said.

Jason's sermons were always so compelling, he spoke with authority and passion that surpassed the other ministers. He'd pace back and forth on the podium, beads of sweat pouring down his temples and his suit jacket thrust aside, exposing his heavyset belly covered by a white button-down shirt, sticking to his skin from more perspiration. I racked my brain for who I might be holding a grudge against. I wasn't one to hold grudges, and I didn't feel like I needed to repent for anything in particular. As Jason pressed the people; however, I

49

realized I had to repent to someone of something. I finally left my seat to find a sibling who I'd been quarreling with. I knew that our relationship was often snippy with each other, and I was sometimes a little bit of a smart ass when I could be kinder. So, I sought her out and hugged her, confessing that I really loved and respected her and I would try to do better. On my way back to my seat, I had to weave through people hurriedly trying to find the one they needed to confess to. I noticed a line of people in front of one person. I moved in close to see who so many people had a beef with. It was the pastor's daughter. I heard people confessing one after the other how they were jealous of her.

Violet Coleman was in her 40s with a beautiful, soulful singing voice, a heavyset black woman with paler skin than most, gorgeous hair and her head held high. A large gaudy necklace hung from her solemn expression as she graciously allowed all the women to repent before her. We linked eyes, and not knowing what else to do, I drew closer to her and shook her hand, saying the usual greeting that was said whenever you greeted another in the church, "God bless you." She didn't smile, she just repeated my words, looking down at me as I spoke, waiting for me to say something else, but that was it. I'd never been jealous of her; she was just someone to revere, so I moved along, allowing the line I'd cut in front of to resume its motion.

Finally, the day came, the day that Brother Coleman was to finally be healed. He would be there preaching; it was the day. I was so eager to have Brother Coleman healed, but I would rather have words directly from God than hear a sermon from Brother Coleman. Was that terribly wrong of me to think? My captive wish that I hadn't dared voice was made reality as the night unfolded. Jason preached as we waited with bated breath and excited praises to God for Brother Coleman to walk through those ballroom doors. Jason was more excited than ever before; he ran up and down the aisle ways, exhorting the people, laying hands on people, filling people with the Holy Spirit. At one point, Sister Martin, a quiet little black lady, who was an icon as the only woman in a wheelchair who consistently came to church, at Jason's loud declaration for her to rise, she did. It wasn't common knowledge at the time, but apparently, she could rise sometimes. Whatever her ailment, she wasn't fully paralyzed. I'll say it again though, that wasn't common knowledge. What was common knowledge was she was a woman in a wheelchair, and she had stood up. There was a wave of applause throughout the room. There was a strange energy in the room, an electric atmosphere that stayed until past midnight. Past midnight, when it was obvious that Brother Coleman wouldn't be coming that night, the convention ended, and Coleman was still sick.

Why had the prophecy not come to fruition? Why was he not healed? The next few days, as life went back to somewhat normal and I slept normal hours, eating and drinking in the appropriate quantities once again with my sweet new French friend, I lived in a blur. I was bewildered, shocked, and disappointed. How could God say He was going to do something and then not do it? I wondered at the nature of God.

When the usual service schedule of Sunday and Wednesday resumed, we were all filled in. Brother Jason Baker told us that Brother Coleman was not healed because we had such little faith, and this conclusion was echoed by other ministers. God hadn't healed him because of our unbelief and lack of prayer. I thought about it; I had been praying; I'd been praying for Brother Coleman to be healed ever since I could form words into a prayer. Also, recently, my prayer had been tinted with expectancy; I knew I could trust that God would be healing him soon. Or at least, that is what I thought, but that apparently wasn't enough.

Obviously, I needed to have more faith still. They told us that the faith of a mustard seed could move mountains, and I felt that my faith was greater than that. I had such faith; it never crossed my mind that God wouldn't heal him. I simply knew He would. I was confused; how could I have even more faith than that? "Oh Lord, help my unbelief," I prayed, "show me what we can do so that you will fulfill your promise."

A prayer chain was started, and on the bulletin board outside were hour time slots that you and your household could sign up to pray, so that every moment of every day, Brother Joseph Coleman would be prayed for. So, we signed up; I signed up. Praying for an hour for the same person seemed redundant, but we needed God to hear us. We needed God to fulfill His promise.

The summer turned to autumn, and the usually scheduled youth retreat was to be held in October. I was so excited; this was only my second retreat, and I was expecting great things. Again, there was a prophecy that Brother Coleman would be healed. Even though it was a 'youth' retreat, the age range was upped by five years to allow more of the desperate people to attend. My family dropped my oldest siblings and me off, and we set about finding our various rooms. I was excited to discover that I was bunking with several of my close friends. Friends were coming in by bus, and as the buses arrived, I waited eagerly outside the cabins to see my friends' faces. Soon, I was in a circle of seven or eight girls, merrily chatting away the early evening as people walked around us. I vaguely heard someone walking by saying something about us needing coats for fear of catching a cold. I had on a tight maroon false denim jacket, scarf and hat, so I was definitely warm.

Then suddenly, our little circle was interrupted as a familiar voice cut through the air, "Did you hear me?" All of us went silent, and a couple of the girls made way for Sister Violet to cut into our little group. She repeated her question, "Did you hear me?" I looked frantically around me and then realized she was looking at me.

I responded sheepishly, "Are you talking to me?"

She spat the words back at me, "Yes, I'm talking to you, and how dare you be so disrespectful!"

"What...?" I heard ringing in my ears, and I felt nauseous.

"I can't believe you. What's your name?" I desperately tried to pry the name off my lips.

"Charity," I managed to say, feeling that as I let out my name, I exhaled the breath inside my poor lungs.

"I know who you are," she squinted, "you are a Rissler." I blinked. I couldn't move. My friends were suddenly intensely fascinated by their shoes. The world was caving in around me. "I've never known someone so disrespectful. When I am talking to you, I want you to respond. I said, get on a coat!"

"I - I didn't know that you were talking to me; this is a jacket...." I tripped over my words.

"That isn't a coat, and you did hear me, you should be ashamed of yourself!"

Then as quickly as she had appeared, she was gone, but the ringing in my ears wasn't. No one talked and time moved in slow motion. I turned slowly around and dragged my feet in the direction I thought my room was. I heard the wind and the gravel under my feet as my eyes clouded over. One of the girls who I barely knew raced after me and put her arm around my trembling shoulders. "I, I really didn't hear her the first time; I didn't know she was talking to me and I didn't mean to be disrespectful...I thought this was warm enough." Huge tears escaped my eyes as I blinked.

"I didn't really hear her at first either, and I would have thought that would be fine too..." was all she could say, lest she speak against the authority of Sister Violet, so she let me lean on her and accompanied me to my room, where I found the farthest corner bunk, pulled the blanket over my head and cried myself to sleep.

The next day, I was far more rested than any of my friends as I had gone to bed at seven, and anything other than a late night at youth retreat just didn't happen. I tried to block out the previous day's experience with Sister Violet and double-checked myself in the mirror as I started my day. No one would catch me without a coat.

At lunch, one of the days, I found a friend of mine sobbing. I asked her what was wrong and I noticed the same frantic shakiness in her voice that I'd heard in mine a few days prior. I embraced her; she told me that Sister Violet had rebuked her for wearing leggings under her skirt. "I thought," she sobbed, "that this was okay, but she said I should have known better. She said that leggings aren't allowed which I knew, but it's cold and I thought it was fine…"

I agreed wearily, "If anything I'd think it would be more modest…Maybe she didn't think it was right because it's cute? It looks really modest, but someone might wear it who didn't believe what we do." Then I explained what had happened to me a couple nights prior, embraced her, and helped her back to her room.

My sister Hope was also rebuked. She had gotten up early to make the most of the retreat time, and to get the most time possible with some of her best friends, which she only saw every few months. Not wanting to wake people in her room, she left the light off and used a flashlight to gather her things. Later, she was called into a room with the women elders (Sister Violet and Brother Rece's wife and a few other superior women in the church).

"It was said that this morning, you were trying to wake people up by shining flashlights in their eyes."

"Oh, no. I just didn't want to wake anyone up…" Hope responded.

"What were you doing up so early?"

"I was meeting up with some friends…" was her truthful, sheepish response, which if you knew Hope, showed how very responsible she was, but not knowing Hope, you could think that the reason she was getting up so early might be to meet up with a boy. My siblings and I were raised by our parents to be honest, seek truth, and integrity. Therefore, to think that she might be making up a story was to insult in a very deep way. Sister Violet and the other sisters had already formed among themselves a story about what she had been doing that morning, and that was the rebuke they were prepared to give. What she said wasn't heard, and instead, all the sisters proclaimed their great disapproval in Hope Rissler, the one they thought was old enough to be with older people in the same room. They voiced how very shameful and childish her shining flashlights in people's eyes and parading around before hours was.

I wonder, looking back at how something so looked forward to, and so 'enjoyed' such as the youth retreat, could also deeply wound and hurt me, my family, and my friends. Then again, however, the answer is clear. Where closeness and trust are present, the weight of broken trust becomes heavier when it weighs upon you. You would imagine that trust broken would make us less revere the one rebuking us, especially when the rebuke didn't make sense. The thought that those in authority could be wrong was so unthinkable; however, that even though we knew they were wrong, we also knew that they were right. We embraced the paradox and took the guilt and shame upon ourselves, rather than think that the person telling those things was misinformed or harsh or mean. Instead, I felt a personal sting, as though God knew I needed a rebuke, and whether I really needed to wear a heavier jacket, or had heard Violet, or been disrespectful was beside the point. I felt, whether consciously then or not, that something must have been wrong with me, and that she was right in rebuking me. I needed to make myself right before God.

Brother Coleman wasn't healed during that retreat, despite our fervent prayers. I wondered whose repentance was blocking his healing, and whose lack of faith was preventing God from fulfilling His promise. Was it me? I found myself saying, "If Brother Coleman isn't healed tonight..." And hearing the gasps of disbelief from my friends.

"How can you say that!? He is going to be!"

"I know," I corrected myself, "I know that he is, but God changed His mind before; I'm saying if it's not time yet, if it's not God's will yet..." I don't remember what the end of my sentence was or if I even finished it, but as time went on, I began doubting my once firm faith in God. I knew I believed in Him, but I was told that if I truly believed Him and 'His' promises, that He would fulfill His promises.

So, I tried to believe Him more, as I realized that God couldn't have been wrong in His promise, so it must be true that I was wrong, that I didn't believe enough. So, I guarded every thought and didn't let myself think, not being vulnerable with myself for a moment lest I find myself admitting that the first time I believed what I thought was God's Word it was with all my heart, I didn't know if I had more heart to believe in Him with.

Everything comes to an end, and as Brother Coleman grew worse and our prayers grew more exasperated, I prayed a prayer in one of my hour time slots where I shouted and got angry and pleaded with God. I really wanted to break through to Him. I felt a very clear answer. I saw the light through the lace curtain and felt a peace rush over me. Then I heard God's words in my heart, "It will be okay." That wasn't the answer I wanted. I tried to correct it, 'So you'll heal Brother Coleman...?' But God gently whispered in my heart again, "It will be okay," and then there was peace again.

I remember one winter morning in early 2012. I'll never forget walking on that cold tile, barefoot into the kitchen where siblings' searching eyes looked from my sleepy face to another in the room as one of my siblings said quietly,

"Has someone told Charity?"

"Told me what?"

I searched all the faces in the room for what felt like an eternity until someone answered, "Brother Coleman died."

4

The Death of an Apostle

So that we may no longer be children, tossed to and fro by the waves and carried about by every wind of doctrine, by human cunning, by craftiness in deceitful schemes.

Ephesians 4:14 (ESV)

"Oh." Everyone in the room watched my face. I felt no strong grief despite what one would imagine. Part of me felt shocked, and then there was another involuntary feeling as a heavy weight lifted off my shoulders.

"When?"

"This morning."

"Okay."

Suddenly, time moved faster. I remember so little from the following months, things were confusing; no one knew all the things I wanted to know. Answers were short and questions were plenty. Jason Baker was nowhere to be found; years later, I heard he'd gotten a job as a chef, I also heard a rumor that he had 'works well under pressure' on his résumé, but strangely as he left, a lot of the pressure left with him.

As ministers scrambled to pick up the pieces of the church, Peter Edwards, the tall British man, preached an iconic sermon that would go down in the church's history. Everyone was suddenly aware that Jason was a false prophet. All at once, we were told that he was a liar, an occasional drunk, a gambler, coke addict, and an all-round charlatan. People were hurt, how long had these things been known? Why was he allowed behind the pulpit? Peter Edwards had answers; his words were perfectly refined like polished glass. He told the people that all that had happened was God's will. He had asked questions about Jason, but Brother Coleman had insisted Jason was trustworthy. So, he wasn't wrong for backing Jason because Brother Coleman had cleared him, and just like Brother Coleman followed Brother Branham, so he and his fellow ministers followed Brother Coleman. Does that mean Coleman was wrong? Well, could somebody ever be truly wrong if it was for our testing? Did he know what he was doing? Who could know? Brother Peter said these words in his beautiful accent, worked the people into a tizzy, and even clicked his heels together on the podium. No one had done anything wrong, and we would be moving on with our lives. He proclaimed that he and the other ministers had nothing to apologize for.

There needed to be a new pastor. Peter Edwards was the pastor of England. Pennsylvania and New York's pastor had been Brother Coleman. Who could fill such shoes as those? Someone temporarily stepped up as they nominated a man to vote on; Brother Moretti, a short, white-haired man, who was the only one left in the church who also remembered William Branham's sermons in person. He would be the new pastor, after a vote of course, but with no other candidates, he was soon in office.

He didn't preach like the other ministers; he preached more Bible stories than the hidden mysteries, but he didn't need to preach all those things, so long as he knew them, and could announce other ministers. It seemed as though they just needed someone they could control. Other ministers were appointed too; one minister had just got out of prison after serving a few years.

There had been a scandal when I was a child, as I grew up I pieced together some parts. Apparently, one of the ministers in the New York branch was a part of a Ponzi scheme. The ploy was an investment company that had a huge rate of return—something upwards of ten percent—too good to be true. I don't know if the company was explicitly endorsed from the pulpit, but everything shy of that, at the very least. Ministers are friends with other ministers, that's the way those things usually work. That being said, so much of the ministry was tied up in the business. Everyone who was anyone and had a red cent to count was investing. My parents put in their small, but ever so precious retirement fund, which was the fruit of blood, sweat, and tears. For one reason or another, people had gotten suspicious, and some people, after putting in quite a lot of money, decided to back out. The money was disappearing, so when people wanted out, others were convinced to opt-in, to give the illusion that everything was running smoothly, new money would be given to those who wanted out.

Eventually, the secret got out, and a lot of people spent real jail time or lesser time depending on how involved or informed that particular person was. Brother Coleman's son spent a few years in prison. The ones who were appointed to the Pennsylvania leadership had spent some time, but we were assured that the prosecution was ill-founded and that they were men of upright character.

There were other affairs to sort out apart from a new pastor—the finances. Now, there is something you need to understand. Although the Pennsylvania branch of Brother Coleman's church was more on the middle-class side of the spectrum, the New York branch was wealthy. Of course, there were some wealthy tithing members in Pennsylvania too, but in

New York, the gross incomes were simply far higher. Tithing was highly encouraged. Not tithing 10% was highly frowned upon. So, I don't know numbers, but between the humble 200 members in Pennsylvania and close to 300 in New York, there was income coming in. Even I tithed the few dollars I made as a preteen.

So, where did that money go? Nowadays, many churches keep accurate records of such details so that church members can see where their money went. However, this church was a little behind the times. They hadn't needed those records because, of course, they would steward the finances well. Besides, Brother Coleman was in charge of that.

But surprisingly, we found that among the church staff salaries, convention hosting, and plane trips for ministers to visit conventions hosted in other countries, tithes were also being used to, as I recall, pay six-figure salaries for each of Brother Coleman's married daughters, who had no official role in the church apart from being the minister's daughters. I realize this number may be incorrect, but it was approximately

100,000 dollars for two people who did not officially work on the church staff.

When the incoming funds were reallocated, and new jobs found for those precious dollars, the remainder of the Coleman's family left. Whether it was due to that fact, the new leadership, or something else, I know not.

In June 2012, the second eldest of my 12 siblings got married to a British gentleman. The fact that my sister had dated him for about seven years including engagement (the length of courtship being drawn out because of distance, college, and career) meant that it was long anticipated. Everyone from the church was invited, and Brother Edwards, the pastor from England, flew in. The wedding served as a splitting point, some people had wanted another person to be the pastor, some people thought that Coleman wasn't really an apostle, and some people wanted to pay tithes to the Coleman family. Most of the people who were leaving held out until the long-awaited Rissler wedding—which was a grand affair—and then they left.

Growing up, I learned to read very late, around age nine, which put me behind in my homeschooling. To compensate, I put in twice as many hours, and by 2012, I had caught up to my peers, putting me in high school. My brother, John, who I greatly respected, asked me how school was going and I explained how I'd been working extra hard, and had caught up.

"What if you keep working just as hard?"

"What do you mean?"

"Well," he mused, "you've been going twice the speed to catch up to your peers, what if you didn't slow down?"

A light went on in my eyes.

"I'd finish high school in two years instead of four," I exclaimed.

"I don't see any good reason not to do that," he said. He had a point. I kept the speed, and dove into my studies.

I was 14 that year, and up to that point in my life, I had said boys were stupid. With my sister getting married, I began to wonder if I were ever to date or marry, who would it be?

There didn't seem to be anyone for me. Out of the three boys around my age at my Pennsylvania church, one was still several inches shorter and a couple of years younger, one was more liberal than I was comfortable with, and another was my second cousin. So, I thought to conclude that I would simply never marry, but instead, I did some investigation and after a thorough perusal of various church families around the world, the answer was clear, I'd marry Brother Edwards's youngest son. He was my age and from a respectable family. He was a little chubby from the one photo I saw, but what could you expect from a fourteen-year-old boy? I knew there were a couple of other eligible boys my age, but my family already had close ties with the Edwards family, so it appeared to be feasible.

One evening, on a ride back from church, my older brother John asked if I liked anyone, I said, "Well, I don't really like anyone, but I think if I did, I know who it would be," and I disclosed the name.

"I knew it," he said. "He's the best candidate, and you deserve the best." I shifted happily in my seat.

"Thanks, John." And that was the moment my knowledge of the boy I didn't know, became a crush on the boy I didn't know.

The next several years were grueling for me; I poured myself into my studies. I planned on starting college at sixteen. When I was still fourteen in the winter of 2012, and when my crush on Leo Edwards was as strong as ever, my brother John and I set out to go to England to visit Faith and her husband who had been married about six months.

Tickets across the pond are rather expensive, but when I wasn't in the troves of studying, I was taking care of my little doll resale/restoration business I was running on eBay which I had started years prior. When I was 11 years or so, my friends were absolutely obsessed with the gorgeous American Girl dolls which had a price tag of about $100—brand new. I wanted to join in the fun, but at that time, I had seventy dollars to my name. So, I began to feverishly watch eBay for the doll I wanted to be at that low price. In my quest, I would see other dolls fall below that price, but not the one I wanted. It dawned on me that since it was so rare that the dolls fell that low, if I were to buy the doll that I didn't want that was underpriced and sell it for what they usually went for, then I'd be able to afford the doll that I wanted; so that's what I did. I bought a doll that came with outfits, and when it arrived, I listed the doll and different outfits separately. I made a thirty-dollar profit from that first doll, which put me at over my goal. I knew then that I could afford the doll I wanted, but I no longer wanted it. I had gotten such a high from making my own money that I wanted to keep doing that vs. playing with a doll. So, I had an eBay tab open right next to my homework screen, which I set to refresh every five seconds. If a deal popped up, I calculated in my head what I could resell each piece for, and I'd buy it within ten seconds of it appearing.

Then I'd fix up the dolls, separate dolls that had been sold together, clean them, sort their accessories, fix their damaged hair and take beautiful pictures with a white backdrop, documenting carefully any imperfections. That's how I, a 14-year-old, had the money to go to England, because of the effort I'd poured into my business as a preteen and then young teenager.

Aphia had come that past summer too; her English was now fluent after a couple of summers at our home. I was eager to visit her in her element; she had no idea I'd be coming—her parents had wanted it to be a surprise. John and I arrived at the airport and jumped on a train to get out of London. I remember I was wearing a green blouse and a black beret because I thought I knew what fashion was, and a denim skirt that was frayed from dragging on the ground. The train arrived at our stop; I recall a suitcase wheel began to jam under the weight of my overpacked suitcase as we pulled our luggage along the muddy sidewalks. We were to be in Europe for a whole month, so I had packed over fifty pounds of clothes and art supplies. There was no car to greet us because our flight got in at the middle of the day when Faith's husband was at work, and Faith was so new to driving on the opposite side of the road, that she didn't feel comfortable picking us up safely. So, we eagerly met Faith at the door of their cute little condo set into the side of a hill on a little English road. As one might expect for England, it was cloudy (some might even say a little dreary), but I was welling up with excitement, as it felt so long since I'd seen my sister.

I thought that one day I would live there, in a little house like my dear sister had taken up with her British husband. I envisioned attending the church that they both attended. When we visited The Message church in England, I recall seeing Sister Edwards and wondering if she would be my future mother-in-law. I walked over to her and she smiled at me. She was quiet but very sweet to me. I remember thinking that Brother Peter Edwards was lucky to find such a gem of a wife. John was dating a girl in that church too, so the thought that I would stay in the states was more far-fetched than moving to England once I was done with college. I was there for several weeks, spending Christmas with them, and then left for France by myself. During that time, I was fortunate enough to see Brother Edwards, and have conversations with him; however, conversations with his son were harder to come by. Gender segregation was always a very real thing. The only way John had gotten to know the girl he was dating was because she was the best friend of my sister Hope.

John's dating interest, her younger sisters, and their friends quickly became friends of mine. I wanted to tell them about my crush, but I soon realized the imprudence of it as I found that I wasn't the only one who thought that Leo was the one for her. The younger sister of my brother's girlfriend had come to the same conclusion and was constantly teased for it. I kept silent on the matter, and as funny and sweet as she was, I thought it far more probable that I'd marry him than her, but at 14, and her 15 (therefore, a year older than him), I didn't see any point in making a fuss about it. No doubt her heart would be broken at some point, but that wasn't my place. I didn't join in on the teasing, because I didn't want to encourage something that was never going to take place. In my mind, it was more appropriate for me to marry Leo, and I was pretty sure that all the adults who had given it any thought felt the same.

Despite the segregation, I did get to shake Leo's hand. There was a point during every service in which we greeted one another, and whoever was sitting right in front or behind you was supposed to shake your hand. So, it happened, I had some kind of social interaction with him other than getting to know his parents. We shook hands, and boy, what a handshake. I heard that Sister Edwards asked about me afterward, my age, and said she'd never seen her son's face get so beet red. I felt that I had left as much a mark as I could. I didn't expect him to make any move on me, nor would it be proper if he had, after all, I was 15. If he hadn't known of me before, now he was at least aware of my existence.

Christmas came, and Aphia's parents asked that I break the news to Aphia on the phone. They had just told her that they had a surprise for her and that somebody on the phone would break the news to me. So, they handed the phone to her, and I, still back at my sister's house, eagerly explained, "It's

Charity!" I could hear her almost hyperventilating on the other end of the line.

"What! Am I going to visit you?"

"No, I'm going to visit you!" I replied.

"When?? You're coming to Europe?"

"I am already in Europe—in England; I'm leaving tomorrow to join you there; I'll be staying for ten days." The happy dance in her voice was unmistakable; she was ecstatic! The day after Christmas, I hopped on a train with my huge suitcase to be in the little French cottage for ten days. I had painted a little picture of her family, which I was eager to present to them. Oh, and how I longed to see Aphia again. My twin—we'd taken to call each other twin since someone asked if we were twins in the first summer she spent with us. We were so close that she really felt like an adopted family member, and I couldn't wait to see her.

I eagerly learned French words to try and communicate the bare minimum with her friends from church. I talked about my crush on Leo, and she talked about hers. She had settled on one of Brother Merten's sons. An excellent choice, really the only one that would make sense for her since there were no eligible French men at her church there in Paris. The only other lad who would do for my treasured friend was Leo. She was taking the other one who I didn't really know much about, but also a pastor's son.

You see, dear reader, as a fourteen-year-old, I thought I knew how my life would play out. I thought I would marry one of the pastor's sons, and Aphia would have followed suit with one of the others. I was so completely naive, but my thoughts were well founded. In my childhood, the full spectrum of potential future suitors was laid out, and unless some new family started coming to church (which was so rare) or one of the unknown foreigners from the non-English speaking countries learned English, those were my only options.

I returned from that trip in January 2013, that year is a blur in my memory, and I don't recall what happened. I think it is safe to say that my school workload may have something to do with the gap in my memory. I met my ambitious goal markers for finishing high school early, and in the spring of 2014, I decided to take a few college credits while I finished up high school. My first college class was an art class; I remember clearly when my professor called out my name from the roster.

"Charity?"

"Here."

"Do you have a Faith and Hope too?" he joked, alluding to the scriptural passage of 1 Corinthians 13, or as an artist, it may have been the classical paintings which personified those virtues that came to his mind. I don't know which.

"Yes," I replied, knowing it was a jab but answering plainly with the ironic truth.

"Yes, I do; they're my sisters, along with Grace and Mercy." He consciously blinked.

"Uh. Really?"

"Yes."

"Well, that's weird," he acknowledged with a squint as he called the next name.

That professor made fun of me for my style and long braid of hair. He tried out many different nicknames for me including hair, braid, and skirts. Finally, he settled on Paris because of my French beret, my recent trip to Paris, and (I flatter myself) my artistic talent.

He wasn't the only one who tried nicknaming me and poking fun at me for my abnormal culture; I didn't take it personally though. I didn't make friends at college that semester, maybe it would have been difficult for me, but that wasn't why I didn't make them. I saw college as a means to an end; I needed a degree, I had a community, and I didn't care what any of the people thought of me, except the professors, because I needed them to give me an A. My older siblings had made, as far as I know, straight As. So, I concluded that an A was the only acceptable grade for someone in my family to make and continued to push myself to meet the high expectations I perceived.

I turned up my nose at people; I was a quiet girl who sat in the corner of the library, but the front of a class. I was successfully the teacher's pet in all of my three classes that semester and successfully made no friends.

I was chatty with a girl who sat next to me in speech class though. I wouldn't call her a friend, but she also cared about getting a good grade and would sit up front with me. She reeked of cigarette smoke every time she came into class. She needed to graduate as well, so she could get a better job and provide for her kid. I respected the fact that she was a full-time student in school and worked, including taking care of a kid, but mostly, I pitied her. She was open about her faith with me.

"I'm what you'd call a heathen," she said pointedly, I wasn't at all shocked, I knew the world was a strange place. She asked me about my faith as well.

"Well, I'm a Christian," I said, hesitating.

"Why do you wear skirts?" she followed up, "Is that part of the Christian faith?"

"Well, I believe in a man called William Branham who was the prophet for our age. He did a bunch of miracles and prophesied a bunch of things. The dress code is part of that faith, setting apart oneself from the world. The dressing like this is such a small part of what I believe, but we do believe in dressing more modestly." I could tell I lost her at, "...A man called William Branham...," but she smiled politely and nodded.

"That's interesting," she commented. I remember feeling mildly embarrassed at the exclamation of faith I expressed to the heathen woman, but I took comfort in what I had heard because I could recall the teaching of my childhood. *The world won't understand it, because they aren't chosen. We are the chosen people, so it doesn't matter what they think.*

The semester came to a close, and I got an A in all my three classes.

5

The Mirage is Fading

If any of you lacks wisdom, let him ask God, who gives generously to all without reproach, and it will be given him.

James 1:5 (ESV)

After my semester was up, I buckled down to finish 12th grade. I was excited to finally be done with high school and not have to log everything I did that was of some educational value every day. I was planning on revisiting England late that summer, and I was thinking a lot about my future. I perceived that I had a minute influence on the people around me and very little control of my circumstances (which I understand is a normal feeling for a teenager). I had asked my parents that if I got one of the scholarships I was applying for, perhaps I could be permitted to live on campus. They gave me a flat no, "Until you're 18, you're living in this house, and going to a college close by."

Because I perceived so few options for myself, I meticulously plotted to control everything I possibly could in my circle of influence. I planned out each moment of every day. Eager to make my life as good as it could be, given my circumstances, I read every self-help book I could get my hands on and continuously called up my siblings who I held great respect for. I wanted to make myself the best possible version of me—academically, spiritually, physically, financially—in everything that I had control over, I would fine-tune to perfection. They talked a lot about perfection in church; they said there were seven steps to perfection—faith, virtue, knowledge, temperance, patience, godliness, and brotherly kindness. The way this was illustrated was by a pyramid, and at the top, after adding all these things to ourselves, we would receive the Holy Spirit. In the final stage, we would be crowned by the capstone of love, made perfect.

As a child, I pondered what that could mean, how was one to go about implementing such a system? Now, one of my favorite books as a teenager was *The Autobiography of Benjamin Franklin,* which I read several times. I related to this man because he was self-made and had a similar goal—though his strategy for perfection was lacking a crucial point; he didn't know about 'the seven steps'. Benjamin Franklin had, at one point in his life, fancied that he might be able to make a roadmap to perfection, so he sought about bettering himself one trait at a time. The first thing on his list of character corrections he wished to make in himself was not to speak in excess but to hold his tongue when his words were not necessary. He planned to do a full week with no misgivings in this resolution. Once he got to a full week with no mistakes, he would add the next trait, and so forth until he'd reached mastery in all the traits, but he never got past the first week with no errors, so he restarted repeatedly. He did confess that although he found it impossible to be perfect with his efforts, he did notice that the bad habit he had (talking in excess to the point of others exasperation) considerably improved. He had more discipline in that area, even if he fell back into it.

I found Benjamin Franklin's efforts fascinating; I wished to do the same. Perhaps with the seven steps to perfection and God's divine intervention, perfection would be reached. In any case, I found another one of Franklin's points in his autobiography most true. He said that the one thing that it was impossible to completely correct was pride. For if you could be fully humble in all things, human nature would dictate that you would be proud of your humility—a truly impossible feat. As for me, I didn't try to be humble, for knowing that it was impossible to be fully humble, that is the one thing I didn't try to correct in my behavior. The irony was that while I didn't think that was possible, I did think that perfection might be. The only time I would make efforts to correct my pride would be when it showed itself as arrogance that put other people down. Even that effort was minimal, and really only there to satisfy my desire to be well-liked.

I had read through the entire Bible by way of a reading plan and was on my second time around. I always followed the rules, the only rule I would not follow was watching PG-13 movies my parents didn't know about, which was a conviction neither William Branham nor Brother Coleman preached about. Apart from that, I thought myself to be a saint. Older sisters at church would stop to talk to me and compliment me on the way I'd styled my hair or how I style my outfits. Many of my friends wore things that were mildly questionable, stuff like a neckline that showed a bit of the collarbone or a skirt that sometimes when walking, exposed some knee. I made a point of doing all my research, for if all of William Branham and Brother Coleman's words were to be revered equally, I was going to make sure I knew every rule and doctrine. I wanted to decipher the words that were a mystery in my youth. People took notice of my meticulous efforts in this area, as well as my academic accomplishments, and my overall desire for wisdom and knowledge. I was going to be above reproach in every way.

During my first semester, when my professors weren't teasing me about my name or many siblings, they praised me tirelessly, knowing when they called on me, I would know the answer. My peers in school (not by age), had a strange kind of respect and regard for me, while my peers in church would listen with bated breath when I told my stories from school. None of that praise or attention could satisfy me; I was restless, eager to make my mark and impress the world. I constantly competed with myself, striving to do better than yesterday. I was an optimistic dreamer, working hard for everything that came my way. The word, 'lucky' became my pet peeve. "You're so lucky to have the opportunity to finish high school early!" (I worked twice the hours for this...)

"You're so lucky you can draw so well." (I haven't always been this good, I've spent countless hours practicing.)

"You're so lucky you got to go to Paris." (I paid for it.)

"You're so lucky to have such healthy hair!" (I take really good care of it.)

The past couple of years, I'd been writing a book. It was a religious thriller about the peer pressures of high school, which lifted the veil between the demonic realms. Ruth had first introduced me to this obscure genre of books, and after reading many of the novels, I set about writing mine. She eagerly held me accountable, asking every Sunday at church if I had written more and could email her the draft to read.

I looked forward to the day when I could move to England and start living life there. I'd done the research and those moving to England had to meet certain income requirements, or be married. I didn't like the idea that I would have to marry into England, even though I simultaneously had a crush on a boy from England. I detested the idea that I would need anyone else. After all, what if I ended up being like one of the older single women in the church? No, that would not do. I needed the option of moving to Europe or wherever it was that men were, on my own terms.

Life was good, or at least, I thought it was as good as it could be, given my circumstances. More specifically, I thought it was as good as I could make it be. I was a self-made sixteen-year-old. I remember one day sitting in my sister Hope's room, and she was talking about how unhappy she was. I wore a hollow smile every day, but today, I was honest with her and myself.

"I understand," I said.

"I'm not happy. In fact, I feel this emptiness inside. Shouldn't I, of all people, be happy? Don't I have every reason to be happy?"

"I didn't know you felt that way—I thought you...?"

"Because I joke and smile, you think I'm happy? I don't know what I am."

The conversation abruptly ended as she left with my mom for an appointment. The house was eerily still. "God..." I whispered into the silence, "can you hear me?" The aura of the environment never changed. I swallowed hard, "God, do you ever listen to me? Would you, for just a second?" I looked at the ceiling, with no measure of civility, "God, everyone thinks I'm so close to you, and rightly so, I read the Bible all the time and Message books." I glanced meaningfully at Hope's bookshelf, which was a mirrored image of mine in the next room; covered in notebooks, self-help books, and The Message books.

"God, I do everything you require of me. If you would be close to anyone, wouldn't it be me?" The silence in the house was unbroken, and my words felt dry, not causing a ripple.

"God!" I shouted, as I blinked, and a tear fell from my eye. I didn't wonder if anyone was home or if they could hear me, I was only concerned about one set of ears.

"God, am I wrong? Do I not read more than most, do I not follow the rules as well as anyone? Yet, all of this, and I feel as though I don't even know the one I'm doing it for. I feel like you don't even hear me when I pray!"

At this point, more tears joined the first few, and I was blinded by their persistence. I began to sob passionately, as I wondered if God would ever listen to me, or where He was. "God, I want you to be present in my life; I want you to listen to me and answer my questions! I'd do anything to hear your voice in my life." There was an interruption to my flow of words, and the question appeared before me, "Would you really do anything, or would you only do something convenient for you?" I felt insulted by this question, in defense I reiterated, "Yes, anything! I'm not just saying that! I'd read the Bible more still, change my career path, stay in the States, pray more, read Message books more, watch sermon archives..." I burst into tears again; I knew the things I was saying were things I had already tried, but if God told me that doing more of those things would be the key to drawing close to Him, I would try harder.

"God. I am willing to do ANYTHING to breach the gap—to get this little emptiness out of my life, anything to feel you close, and find clarity. Tell me what it is..." I couldn't help but wonder at my own words, was I serious, how much did I want God in my life? Desperately. Desperately was the answer.

Then, to prove to God that I was serious, I began to search in my mind what the hardest thing would be for me to do, and it hit me; I thought that if my whole framework of beliefs were wrong, that would seriously be the hardest.

So, I reluctantly said, "God, EVEN if The Message is wrong, even if ALL that is wrong," my mind was screaming, *"How could you even suggest that!? Letting the doubt in again?"*

Since even entertaining a moment of doubting in that church was considered a grave sin, so I quickly added, "I know it's not! But IF…I know it can't be... but IF it was, even that, if that is the thing 'off,' show me, tell me, and I'll change!"

The stillness in the room broke. My tears stopped. I felt that for the first time in a long time, God heard and listened to my words. Almost audibly came a calm reassurance. There were no words in this reassurance, and it wasn't an immediate answer, and I didn't know what I should do. I didn't know when I would see the answer, but I left that conversation with an assurance it would be all right.

A few weeks went by, and I began to forget about that conversation with God. Church was carrying on as usual, but my songs were a little less loud, and my amens were a bit less frequent. One Wednesday night, I remember there being an altar call. This wasn't the usual altar call you'd imagine in a Christian church. Instead, we were asked if we had doubts in our hearts that we needed to repent of. I knew this to be true; I felt guilty that I had, for a moment, suggested that this might not be true, even if it was in a prayer to my Lord and Savior. So, I went up to the altar and prayed a simple prayer, asking forgiveness for my doubt. I remember there were tears on my cheeks, but I don't recollect them flowing from me out of grievance for my sin, more of a confused fear or a frustrated impatience.

I was starting to see that some of the things I thought God was, He wasn't. I always thought He was urging me to do things and then urging me not to do those things, and I was beginning to see that both couldn't be true. I remember when service ended, and the brothers and sisters of the church filed out, someone said they were proud of me and happy that I had gone up to the altar that day. I felt sick to my stomach; I didn't feel that going up to the altar to repent for doubt was something that I needed to do. Had I forgotten the conversation I had with God so recently? Had I forgotten how He had heard my prayer? No, I hadn't, but had He forgotten it?

The next memory in this narrative is a pivotal moment in my life. The details are hazy, but here is what I know. It was late, surely past my bedtime. I was barefoot, and the house was quiet. I crept down the stairs and walked into the kitchen. The lights were dim; one small light was illuminating the countertop. My brother Andrew was there talking with my mom. As I walked in, both pairs of eyes met mine. I went to get a glass, "What?" I said, stopping with it in my hands.

Andrew looked flustered, "Is it okay if I talk about this with Charity?" He looked to my mom, and I piped in,

"Talk about what?" My mom looked away, wiping the already clean countertop with the rag in her hand.

"You can talk about it with her," she said, as she faded out of the scene. I saw Andrew's normally composed face contort as he tried to form the words I so desperately needed to hear; I could feel my heart racing.

"What??"

"Charity," his words hung in the air with every breath, "Charity, I don't think that Brother Branham was a prophet."

The whole room emphasized his words, and I remember hearing other words in my mind as well: "This is it, this is the answer you asked for!" I knew, at that moment, God had answered my broken prayer, "Tell me everything," I said to Andrew, as I poured myself a cup of tea.

6

The Nature of a Prophet

And if you say in your heart, 'How may we know the word that the Lord has not spoken?'— when a prophet speaks in the name of the Lord, if the word does not come to pass or come true, that is a word that the Lord has not spoken; the prophet has spoken it presumptuously. You need not be afraid of him.

(Deuteronomy 13:21-22)

I like to say that I made my decision to leave after much compelling research, but that's only a half-truth. When I look back at the memory, I realize how my heart shifted, and without that shift, prior to seeing the research, I know that no amount of research that I'd been shown or that I had found of my own accord, could have induced me into seeing anything other than something that painted The Message as true. Anything contrary to The Message doctrine would have fallen on deaf ears. That's why the prayer I had with God weeks prior was so vital. It is funny how the facts can't simply change people's minds and opinion. No, it doesn't work that way, especially when this was something I was proud to be a part of and happy to have a future in. I clung so tightly to my beliefs with something known in psychology as confirmation bias; that is to say that I only saw things that confirmed my beliefs. That night, the spell was broken, and I started to see. Telling me that I could make a life for myself outside of The Message would have been like telling a fish to join you in the fresh air. I knew there was a life outside, but that wasn't possible for me, and if it was possible, I had no idea what my future might look like.

On that evening, as I pensively sipped my tea and sat in the basement at Andrew's desk, curled up on an office chair, it was the thing that I hadn't wanted to happen, but it felt right at the same time. Like eating my vegetables or exercising, I knew

I needed this, and while I didn't want it, I also felt a certain peace about it. I'd imagined that when people were leaving The Message, it was because they let the doubt in, tasted what the world had to offer, and lost respect for themselves—that the rules and mockery surrounding their appearance had been too much for them to bear. I assumed that at some point, they wished for acceptance outside of our sphere, and that's what pulled them away from the words they knew to be true. While that may be true of some, I never sat with them to hear their stories, for they were dead to me. Now, here I was, risking alienation, listening to 'blasphemies.'

It was like being an alcoholic that had been in full denial, always surrounded by drinking buddies and unable to hear the truth from a sober person who didn't know how to 'loosen up.' When finally confronted about the severity of their delusion and the degree of the problem, for whatever reason, the blindness is lifted. He knows if it is true, that he's an alcoholic, then that means that he needs to make many changes, forgo the life he wants, slowly and surely and seek out a better way, and that's hard. It's not something he wants, but he knows he needs to, so he listens, and gets a little emotional as he mourns the death of his reality which wasn't what he thought it was. So, I listened, and I learned. I asked questions that felt endless, prompted by awakened humility and broken pride. I knew this was only the beginning. Was William Branham a prophet? That was the framework of what made everything else he said both credible, and a firm foundation worthy of building your life upon. He was a prophet who had been proven by visions and prophecies coming to pass, along with other signs and wonders that vindicated him by God as His chosen prophet for our age. What is a prophet though? Simply put, it is someone who prophesies, but someone prophesying doesn't mean that they are a good prophet. I could prophesy that Joe Schmo will buy a cat tomorrow and maybe he will and maybe he won't. If he does, then it can be said that I successfully prophesied an event. Next, there is quality and quantity. There are specifics that I could prophesy, things like Joe Schmo will buy his cat at 1:30 PM tomorrow, and it will be a calico cat, and he'll name him Spot. That prophecy is harder than the former. Of course, if I made more of such prophecies and all came to pass, that would make me even more credible as a prophet. There are certain fascinating things about being a prophet. So many factors and variables could add or take away from my credibility.

I could manipulate the system though. I could hear about Joe's intention of buying a cat, and that he preferred Calico, and maybe I overheard his daughter saying that she had a cat that she loved that died whose name was Spot. I could have heard her mother say that her husband planned on surprising her with a pet during his lunch hour to surprise her. Knowing such things, I could then fill in the gaps and make a prophecy that would be a little startling even to the parties involved who told me parts of the details.

I could also, after the event took place, say that I prophesied it in even greater detail than I actually did, but people would remember me saying something about the prophecy and would, therefore, stand behind me.

I could also make several prophecies all around the same time, surrounding many different people, the sheer number of prophecies would play the odds in my favor of a prophecy coming to pass. If I were concerned about being a reputable prophet, then naturally, should I prophesy something that flew far from the mark, I could simply never bring it up again.

Why do I say these things? I am trying to explain that the art of being a convincing (false) prophet is perhaps easier than one might think. Someone with a great memory, particularly keen people with skills, and a certain level of discernment, could make a great "prophet," if not tested too much. One might even say that they have the gift of prophecy. So, what about William Branham? The one whom I had built my reality around. Was this man a prophet, and if so, was he a good one?

Before thinking about prophecies of his that perhaps didn't come to pass, Andrew suggested that to start; we could look at the ones that did. I was led to believe that he was prophesying all the time and that those prophecies always came to pass, but when it came down to actually finding such a prophecy that could be proven (both that he prophesied it before the fact, and that it actually happened) was surprisingly arduous. He had most of his sermons on audio recording, on little cassette tapes which had since been digitized and transcribed by his loyal followers after his death. There is, in fact, a search tool for every documented sermon he ever preached, as well as biographies, digitized life records, and comprehensive lists of quantifiable things in his ministry such as prophecies. So, Andrew and I started looking at the core prophecies. When he was a boy, he saw a vision of a bridge being built and men falling off that bridge and dying. Later, he said the event took place, and it was 'in the newspapers all the way across the country and in Canada.' It turns out, with the digitalization of such newspapers, you can search most of the newspapers around that time that are now in the public records. It was nowhere to be found. Had he said it could be found in 'all the newspapers' because it was a bold statement, but one hard for people (at the time) to actually look into because they would have needed to hunt down the hard copies? Could it be that he lied? No, surely not, I wasn't ready to think my idol was capable of that just yet.

There were other known prophecies that came to pass; I thought surely that was a fluke, a mishap where documents had been conveniently lost to discredit him. He was also said to have prophesied the death of Marilyn Monroe, down to the details, but the details were wrong. He said in a vision he had that he saw a beautiful woman die, and a voice said that people would say she died of suicide, but it was a heart attack and apparently, a few days later is when Monroe died. He said she died at 4 AM, and that had been what he'd seen in his vision, and he very well may have seen that, but she didn't die at 4 AM. An autopsy came back showing she consumed enough sleeping pills to kill ten people. So, while you could stretch the truth and say that she may have had a heart attack right after she ingested pills and the actual cause of her death was a heart attack, that would be stretching the truth indeed.[6]

Branham also prophesied that the world would end in 1977, something I hadn't heard about, but sure enough, the quotes supported it, and naturally one could say something absurd like the world did end in 1977, in some way. You could say the world died spiritually in 1977, or that was something he said as a man and not as a prophet; these were the kind of things I continued to tell myself. I could see how truth had a bitter taste in my mouth and how nauseous I started to feel. It couldn't be this obviously wrong? So easily disprovable...Could it? If it could, how did we all believe it for so long?

There were also prophecies that were considered the cornerstone of his ministry and why his words were still relevant. One thing I had lumped in with these prophecies was actually an event that he hadn't actually prophesied, but something that he claimed happened to him. "What about the cloud? The cloud that was in LIFE magazine, the cloud that was the vindication of his message, how could that be disproven?" You see, dear reader, there was a sign so majestic I felt that no one could deny. The day that William Branham went hiking when he would receive revelations from heaven, that day above him formed a cloud so high that it couldn't be a cloud. It was higher than clouds would form—it was 'a ring of mystery' according to LIFE magazine.[7] I thought surely, a sign like that, a cloud like that following him on his journey—if anything were a sign, it'd be that.

"Well, Charity," Andrew pulled up some articles on his computer, "LIFE magazine retracted their statement in the next issue; they solved the mystery of the cloud. There was a rocket launch near the mountain Branham climbed, around the time when he received his revelations. That's why the 'cloud' was able to form so high; it wasn't a cloud at all.

"What about it looking like the silhouette of Christ?" Some people thought that was what the cloud looked like. Andrew cocked his head to one side.

"Does it really look like that, Charity?" I never thought it had, if I was honest. It was really only one of the photos that was reminiscent of Hoffman's painting of Christ's beard.

"Well, not really…"

Andrew continued, "Branham was preaching about it as a 'ring of mystery,' but one sermon where he had planned to preach that, he had a poor print. The printer didn't work, so where the blue sky is, since it was printed in black and white and the paper was blotchy, it looked like a face, so he rolled with it." Andrew pulled up a scan of that very print that had been uploaded to the internet under research about William Branham.

"Oh...that does kind of look like a face," I said, cocking my head and trying to hide my cringe.

"It's kind of eerie, to be honest," Andrew said with upturned eyebrows, "maybe that's why this print was never shown in church." I looked away.

"Yeah...," then under my breath, "a rocket, huh? It was a cloud of rocket smoke all along?"

Andrew hesitated, "It's not just that...because you could still say that the rocket smoke was what God used to vindicate him all the same...but the thing is, it wasn't even where he was on that mountain, even though he said he was standing right below it.[8] The path of the cloud wouldn't have even been seen from where he was when he was there," He pulled up one newspaper after another and traced his finger along a map. "This is where the rocket was, and this is where the LIFE photos were taken, 200 miles away[9]."

"Wait, so it wasn't even there? Why would people say it was there?"

"Yeah, it was so far from there, he wouldn't have even been able to see it from where he was. He would have seen it after...and it's not even the day of that trip; the cloud appeared February 28th, 1963. Branham first made the connection of the cloud with his trip on Nov 10th about eight months later. The trip, though, can be tracked down. He said it happened on the 3rd day of the trip, which would have been the morning of March 8th... Which is, in reality, over a week after the cloud appeared." It didn't add up.

"Then why?" I cut in, leaving my question open-ended, "why do people believe it? Why do people say it?"

"Well, Brother Branham said it, and he showed evidence, dates, and times. That information was just passed on."

"Did no one fact-check?"

Andrew shrugged and sighed, "Well, if they did check, who would believe a fact-checker vs. a prophet of God? It requires you to do the research yourself, I guess."

I sighed too; I knew he was the fact-checker in this case. A couple of generations after the initial words of William Branham, and still, the fact-checkers...Who would give them the light of day?

"That's wrong...How can people not know? How can so many people collectively believe lies like that? Why don't people do their own research?" As I asked the questions, they were more rhetorical than anything, for I knew that I never did research. I just assumed it was all true because everyone around me also thought it true, including people much older and wiser than myself, and surely they would know if it wasn't true. I began to see; however, they were just like me, believing it because everyone around them believed it, and if not now, at one point, there were those who were also older and wiser who they looked up to, who knew it was true. So, we all were sincerely believing lies we counted as the truth.

7

The Summer Tea Party

The steadfast love of the Lord never ceases; his mercies never come to an end; they are new every morning; great is your faithfulness. "The Lord is my portion," says my soul, "therefore I will hope in him."

Lamentations 3:22-24 (ESV)

The weeks and months following the initial couple conversations were followed by more of the same. There were many more conversations with Andrew, some with other siblings, and more research, on my own and with those around me. I count myself blessed that I had siblings nearby at the time to study with.

One Sunday, Andrew brought some points of his research to the new pastor, Brother Moretti, who you'll remember, was voted in after the death of Brother Coleman. Humbly, he presented a few of the points, fitting the role of an inquisitive, concerned, doubter, seeking help. Brother Moretti responded in kind, with elegant reassurance that he would investigate the points presented; that he would do the required readings and answer him. He thanked Andrew for bringing the issues to his attention.

Then came Wednesday, there was a live service. There was never a live service on Wednesdays; this was a big deal. I feel the pits of my stomach knotting themselves up even as I write these words. There was a sermon, if you could call it that—a very passionate one—on 'intellectual spirits'. What's that, you might ask? That is how he referred to my brother. With little tact apart from leaving out my brother's name, he defaced my brother. My dear brother, who in kindness and humility, brought well researched and legitimate questions concerning William Branham, was now being blasted from the pulpit, and the people said amen. Brother Moretti mentioned how somebody (an intellectual demon) had brought up various points, about specific prophecies made by William Branham, and about specifics of the 'Cloud Vindication.' Brother Moretti told of how he was asked to do research, but that he didn't bother—why? Because he was there during the ministry of William Branham. He saw the workings of William Branham; he knew what was true, so why would he look up sites on the internet that were meant to spew lies? He knew because he was there, and he felt the anointing. And the people said amen.

So, here I was, sitting in old pews, watching my friends say 'Amen!' when they preached against intellectual people— people like me. The crazy part is, I couldn't be mad, because I knew that a few months prior, I would have also been saying amen. I would have also avoided the girl who was leaving the church if I knew she was leaving, lest I too 'catch' an 'intellectual spirit.' The ministers too, for the most part, were passionately doing and saying what they thought was right (that's what I'd like to believe anyway). So, if I couldn't be mad, then what I could be was scared, cautious, self-conscious, anxious, and depressed.

The following services I took notes, two lines in each line so that it was so small no one could read over my shoulder. I would say amen more consciously; I would still say it, but only to things that I knew I believed. Things that may have been taken out of context, but that I believed based on a more biblical understanding. There was only so much notetaking I could stomach, especially when dehumanizing things were being said.

I remember a couple of times when I turned my usual side braid into a hiding spot for an earbud. I would put one earbud in and listen to 'Mere Christianity' by C.S Lewis during church. I wanted something to edify me, to spiritually grow me…Not something to tear me down. I remember a deacon approaching me to whisper in my ear if I could move down a few seats to make way for more people, and I didn't know what he was saying. I had to turn my head to the other side, and I've always wondered if he could hear the audio when he was so close to my ear. That was the day I ditched the earbuds and went back to listening to the sermons and taking notes.

I reverted somewhat to the good old days when I was a child, and I'd draw pictures on the inside of coloring pages at church. Only this time, I would draw swirls in the margins of my notebook and practice fancy handwriting on the sermon titles to help the time pass.

I visited England for the second time in the summer of 2014. The first time I visited, I was giddy with excitement and anticipation. I had squealed with delight when the plane took off from the airport in Pennsylvania and had eagerly watched the clouds outside. This second trip was sobering; I went with my dear cousin, Ruth.

My sister, Faith, had a baby since I had last visited her home, so Ruth, Faith's family, and I busied our days with happy walks in the park together. We toured some castles and spent several days at home painting the day away; oh, what a life! However, even when the England days were sunny, there was a storm in my mind which I couldn't find shelter from. To say I wasn't eager to see all my friends again would be a lie, but I felt my world crumbling around me. I asked myself, who am I? Who are these people to me? The English churchgoers were oblivious to the whirlwind inside my head. It was apparent to me that even ministers in the church thought I was as piously devoted as ever.

Faith mentioned a conversation she had with one such minister. They'd been talking about how impressed he was with me, how I'd always take notes—Since it was so uncommon for a young person, he thought it very inspiring. While on that train of thought, Faith turned to an upcoming occurrence relating to a different minister—one I knew well— Brother Peter Edwards. Brother Edwards had invited us over for tea that Saturday afternoon. Faith commented with a nod to me that the Edwards family hadn't asked them to tea before, and that she thought this must be because of me—for me. I exhaled heavily. Why did the renowned Brother Peter Edwards want me for tea? I knew in part, I felt nauseous at the thought, I figured that this was him giving Leo and me an opportunity to meet. I'd dreamed as a silly fifteen-year-old of the days when my courtship with Brother Edwards' son would come to fruition. This was when knowing of each other would turn into us actually knowing each other.

This was the life I had wanted. I remember what I wore that day—a pink, plaid, short-sleeved button up and my long dark denim skirt which always prompted the question from other sisters, "Where did you get that? I would like to find one like that for myself!" My hair was up in one of my signature updos, and my face was blotchy. Also, if I haven't mentioned it earlier, I was a sixteen-year-old, so acne, generally, was an issue for me. It was amplified by stress, and no one was allowed to use any makeup, including a little concealer or powder.

We pulled into the driveway where they had a sweet little cottage surrounded by green grass and the signature of England; muddied paths. We were greeted by the angelic face of Sister Edwards. My heart skipped a beat; this could have been my mother. I swallowed hard as I embraced her, as sisters did. Her eyes spoke in whispers of her pleasure at seeing us. Peter Edwards, of course, was there.

He was, as I may have told, a very tall man but as he stooped down and outstretched his hand, he had a way of making you feel quite his height, even though I was far from it.

"Welcome to our humble home," he smiled, and I felt as though I was in a page of a Jane Austen's book.

"Thank you," I smiled back, my heart was warm, even as my stomach churned. Before I knew what was happening, we were very comfortable in their little garden on cushioned chairs that smelled of morning dew. It was then that I realized Leo and Albert were nowhere to be seen. As though reading my mind, Sister Edwards said offhandedly how they were positively riddled with homework; else, they would have joined us. A bee landed on my ear, and I shooed it away.

"Charity," Brother Edwards said, leaning forward in his chair as he candidly rested his elbows on his lap. "There have been reports…" My stomach knotted as the rest of the garden conversation faded into silence, and his charming face demanded my attention. "…Of doubt in the church…" I hid as much of my face with the delicate teacup as its small frame would permit. He continued, "I wanted to take this opportunity to speak to some of the questions that have been circulating in Pennsylvania and New York. I want to help in equipping you to stand firm in the faith." I nodded and smiled as the world around Brother Edwards faded in and out.

He then began an elegant speech to thoughtfully dispute all the things that I may have heard about. "Firstly, there is the matter of Brother Branham's vindication by the cloud. Some say that it was a rocket, or that it wasn't where it was meant to be at the time. Well, I did some research..." I could tell his points were so thoroughly researched; it made me hold high respect for him. Brother Moretti, when he'd heard these things my brother had said, didn't take the time to do any research. Brother Edwards took time and effort, even though piecing together plot holes in a story is hard when it was fabricated at the start. Defending a lie is tedious work, though it is made easier if you don't know that's what it is.

"Lastly," he said, as his presentation closed, "so much internet research is taken out of context to say what the writer wants it to say." I piped back in, my lips which had been petrified up until this point morphed into words.

I was eager to say something, "Yes, it is so easy to take things out of context, even Brother Branham's quotes or the Bible. You can take words out of context and make the Bible say almost anything; context is a powerful thing." Brother Edwards looked quite in agreement with my words, even though when I said them, I was thinking of the way he and other ministers took scriptures out of context—not about how people on the Internet took things out of context.

At the end of the discussion, Brother Edwards abruptly stood up and outstretched his hand to me, "I'm glad you're still strong in the faith." I mumbled something about how I had no plans to stop following Jesus, with a smile plastered on my face, which was a very non-confrontational response to his statement. I knew, of course, that he thought I was still in The Message, but I didn't know how to start a conversation about where I stood, especially as my whole belief system; The Message, was crumbling around me. My poor sixteen-year-old self had nothing else left to show to this smooth talker before me, but a submissive smile and a nod.

Brother Edwards apparently didn't notice my inner turmoil. He turned to his wife without skipping a beat, "Do you think the lads are done with their schoolwork now?"

She responded in turn, "I'm sure they must be, I'll go fetch them," and since the homework never existed to begin with (which I was told later by one of the boys), she was quickly back with the two of them. Ruth was there, in England with me, and at that little tea party, but I had been too absorbed in the personal sermon Brother Edwards had given me to notice her presence until Brother Edwards said, "I think you all should play table tennis! (They called ping-pong table tennis in England) Two on each side!"

Leo seemed to know what his father was up to, the only two who appeared oblivious were Albert (Leo's older brother) and Ruth. To them, Brother Edwards was innocently prompting a game. To me, it seemed clear, and it seemed clear to Leo as well, "I'm not even good at table tennis, can't we do something else?" Leo piped up.

"No, do have a hand at it, it'll be fun!" he said it with such a jovial leap in his voice, and the verdict was set. Brother Edwards seemed like the sort of man who usually got his way. So, we proceeded to have the most awkward double date that there ever was. Picture it, a garden in England, four young teenagers, who were terrible at ping pong, playing in silence, as the adults eagerly watched from the garden.

My trip to England was coming to an end, and once again it ended by boarding a bus (and ferry) to France. I was always eager to see Aphia, and this was no different. I met her in Paris; she was there with her two sisters who had a flat next to the Notre-Dame (I consider myself lucky to have seen it before it burned down). Aphia and I exchanged a long hug and dance of joy that made all the Frenchmen on the street stare. When we got back to the flat, I couldn't stop smiling. I saw her sisters rush to smash a bug and speak in hushed French tones, "What was that?" I piped up.

"Oh, nothing." They quickly buzzed back. I thought for certain it was a cockroach, but I honestly didn't care.

Aphia and I shared many grand adventures in those few days I got to spend with her. I told her about how I didn't think it would work out with Leo Edwards anymore. I told her about not believing The Message anymore, in little detail. She asked me why and I said I'd had a rough few months and I didn't know that it would be getting better anytime soon. "I almost wish that I didn't know what I know, or that I found it out later, after I could move out from home, or had some right to make my own decisions; as it is now, it's hard." For those reasons I held back telling her any real research against The Message just then, and I headed back to Pennsylvania.

8

The People Said Amen

Even though I walk through the valley of the shadow of death I will fear no evil, for you are with me; your rod and your staff, they comfort me.

Psalm 23:4 (ESV)

Most of my older siblings had moved out by this point, and with my next oldest sibling with a summer internship, there was some time in 2015 where I felt quite alone. I didn't want to burden my younger siblings, and I didn't want to cause a stir among my friends in The Message either.

It was about six months between the time that I knew I was in a cult to the time that I stopped regularly attending. The church was preaching subtly and not so subtly against members of my family—against my siblings for leaving, and against my father for 'not controlling his children.' There was a lot of fear, tension, anxiety, and anger within myself and those around me. The primary reason I kept going was that my dad wanted me to, and told me I had to. My dad is a good parent, he wanted what was best for my siblings and myself, so I can't begrudge him for making me continue; after all, he was doing what he thought was right, and I love him for that.

If it had been up to me at the time, I would have left immediately and started going to a different church or none at all; but I was sixteen, and although at that point, I had already gotten a job and started taking college classes, I was still very much dependent on my parents, and I wanted to respect them. Although it is not the exit route I would have chosen, I know God works all things out for good.

On Sundays, I went to The Message church with my family from about 9 AM to 1 PM, depending on the day. If you've forgotten, it was a 45-minute drive to the church, and we had to dress up, so it was quite the ordeal. While I continued to go, I didn't tell my friends at church that I didn't believe for several reasons; most prominently, hardship, respect, and fear. So, in the crowded room, I felt very alone. The sermons took a theme turn, and there were many about 'intellectual spirits' where they would preach against researching The Message, and although they haven't always been consistent with what they preached, they also said several times that believers of The Message had 'graduated from the Bible.' They preached against people who did research, telling people not to associate with those influences, lest you 'catch' an intellectual spirit and are led astray. They also preached against 'make-believers'; people like me, who cried themselves to sleep at night because they realized they were living a lie. 'Make-believers' as they liked to call us, were people who pretended to believe. When the minister in the pulpit preached against a make-believer, saying that they would be thrown away, like the chaff that is thrown into the fire, useless for the purpose God had set before us, I used to adamantly say "Amen!" The coin flipped however, and I regretted all those times I'd said amen, not knowing who I could have been hurting by believing the things I did.

It was the end of 2014, and I was tired of it, the whole summer I'd tried to gain the privilege of not going. In hindsight, I was in a constant state of flip-flopping between anxiety and depression; my nerves were constantly shot. I feverishly took notes of every sermon, and people's apparent approval of me intensified.

"Sure, some Risslers had fallen away, but would you look at Charity?" During that time, I don't know whose approval I sought...I just felt misunderstood and dehumanized (in sermons) all the time.

After every service on the long ride home, I'd whip out my notebook, fight the car sickness that accompanied any form of reading I did in cars, and talk with my dad. I could see blindness in all his answers to my words. The most recurring and easiest fallacy to bring up would be the pastor(s) saying something to the effect that everything said from the pulpit was inspired and 100% true—that you should believe it without a doubt. I would take a blatantly contradictory statement that was made that day and ask him about it. He would usually respond with, "I don't think they meant it like that." Or, "That's interesting; I'll have to look it up," Or, "I think you're twisting their words, Charity." Most usually though, he didn't respond, and I wondered if he heard me at all. Logically, my argument didn't have any holes, or at least, not ones my dad could properly point out. It wasn't about logic though, for we were encouraged not to think about things too much, lest we doubt it—we were supposed to have faith. If it would be easy to understand (they liked to say), then everyone would have the inspiration, but it was to a select few.

You see, the very nature of the doctrine made little room for considering inconsistencies in the doctrine. So, as I talked with my dad, who had been in this section (the church with Brother Coleman) for over 20 years, and other various Message churches for his whole life prior, all I could do was cry, and pray, and wonder. I knew his mind changing would take a miracle—for anyone's mind to change would take a miracle. Yet, there I was, on the other side, in it, but not of it, seeing a new reality as I looked at the beautiful mirage I'd grown up in.

I knew the things they said about people like me weren't true, things like "that's a demon! If you hear someone speaking against it, walk the other way, that's a demon talking!" Yes, I knew those things weren't true; still, the words stung, especially when my friends said amen.

At some point, I wore down my father's will, and I didn't have to go to services anymore. I'd finally worn down my father, but I still looked the part of a Message believer. I gained my freedom, but was I free?

I remember one convention after I didn't believe it anymore and had managed to earn my freedom. I hadn't been to church in a while, but I came because Aphia was there. I remember feeling very strongly that people knew I was out of it. I was anxious a lot and only attended a few services. Many of which I squandered time in the restroom with a pounding headache.

One time, I ran into an older sister ('Sister' used to mean someone in The Message) in the convention bathroom, she shook my hand, and I smiled at her and said the usual greeting, "God bless you."

Then to my shock, she squeezed my hand harder and grabbed my other hand too, and feverishly wheezed with tears in her eyes, "Come back! Come back to church."

I tried to tactfully pry my hands out of hers as my heart pounded. "I'm going to a church," I said, swallowing the lump in my throat.

"What? You are?" Her eyes bulged out of her head, bloodshot, and confused.

"Yes, a Christian church not in The Message, but I have a strong faith, and I know I'm where I should be," I said, trying to stay composed but shook with confusion at her emotional outburst, and not yet being secure in my faith like I was saying I was.

"Oh, well," she said knowingly, her knuckles no longer white, "I'm praying for you."

Aphia knew I was out; I had the courage to tell her, without telling her any details of why. The Message preached that you needed to cut yourself off from the world—even other Christians, because they are the husk (the part of a wheat harvest that is thrown into the furnace). I knew they were talking about avoiding people like me, and I saw Aphia say amen. I looked at her enthusiastic eyes, and felt intense nausea. I escaped to the bathroom and wept.

Later, I confronted her, with tears in my eyes, "Aphia, do you believe that?" She hardly knew what I was talking about and as I explained it, she jumped to my defense,

"I didn't include you in that group. I know your faith is strong, and you're my friend. I know you have a good character and that whatever you left for, it wasn't so that you could live a life of sin...I know that you must have had real reasons."

"They were talking about people like me though; you realize that, right?" I repeated, "because I'm not in The Message anymore."

"Well, I didn't take it that way, and I wouldn't take it that way. You are my friend." I came to tears again that she would deny that part of The Message to keep loving me.

Yet, I couldn't help but wonder how many of my friends felt that way about me? How many of them were ready to shun me as The Message said? If they all thought I was a demon, there was literally nothing I could do to make anyone, sister or brother think the worse of me. If they were from out of town and out of the loop of gossip and didn't know, they would soon, so I had nothing to lose. My defense mechanism is humor, so I was full of charisma the few days of the convention I was there. So, just like the good old days, the girls crowded around me—not the boys, because gender segregation was still a thing.

I was stopped by a friend from Canada; she had hair near floor length, "Your hair is so long!" I exclaimed, not sure what to think—it was the kind of thing that stopped you in your tracks. I'd always had some of the longest hair in The Message until I'd cut a foot off earlier that summer.

"Thank you," she responded. "It's all thanks to you! I followed all your advice." I hadn't remembered giving her my hair secrets, but here she was, following all of them and a couple of years later, made it really show.

"Wow, your hair is longer than mine now, I think."

"What?" she exclaimed in surprise (My hair was in an updo so that she couldn't tell).

"Oh," I factually explained to her, "I've since trimmed it."

"Oh..." she echoed back, and that was the end of our conversation.

I saw Leo and his brother in a group of guys. I hadn't greeted him yet, though I texted him a decent amount; he was predictably dating Aphia, seeing as I had told him that I no longer believed the teachings of The Message about two years prior. I greeted him, and the group around him scattered. Were they so shocked to see a girl? We had a pleasant conversation, and I shook his hand warmly since hugs were forbidden.

Later, at that convention, I bumped into one of the Mertens's sons; he was friends with David, my second cousin. He started chatting me up with much charm, asking about my life and hobbies. I tried not to sigh audibly. He was a good-looking man, and I knew that if it hadn't worked out with Leo, this would be the next most likely person for me to marry even though I'd never met him before. I think he knew this too; however, it was clear he'd not been informed that I wasn't in The Message anymore. I noted him as a young man worthy of respect, but politely excused myself, careful to be civil but show no interest. The sooner he moved on, the better.

He wasn't the only one not in the know; his sister, who was about my age, clung to me, and I think that she and I would have made good sisters. She told me about her crush— an older man who she perceived was making advances on her. It didn't surprise me that she had a crush on someone eight years her senior, for she was, like me, very mature for her age (in some ways) and in others, very naive. I sympathized with her and told her I didn't know anything about the man. Later, I heard her cry when she saw that he was with another woman much closer to his age. I didn't know what kind of encouragement he had given my poor friend, but I thought it very ill of him.

I remember seeing that the girls got up at five every morning so that they could spend time doing elaborate hairstyles, showering, moisturizing, and anything permissible to make themselves look better. One girl said something about how her skin was so full of acne.

"If your skin isn't clear, I don't know what clear skin is," I said, genuinely surprised at her insecurity.

"YOUR skin is the definition of clear skin. It's so perfect!"

"Mine?" I said without flinching, "is because I'm using a few dabs of concealer on my zits. I break out when I'm stressed." Her eyes widened, for she knew, as I did, that concealer was forbidden.

"So, you see, your skin is very clear." I smiled warmly, and she thanked me for my encouragement.

9

Figuring out College

Having the eyes of your hearts enlightened, that you may know what is the hope to which he has called you, what are the riches of his glorious inheritance in the saints,

Ephesians 1:18 (ESV)

I remember one of my first real friends outside of The Message was a girl named Jenni, who lived in my neighborhood. We'd collaborated before for a Valentine's Day party where we were thrown together because of our artistic talent. I, in my great pride, and because I was in The Message at the time of meeting her, had thought that she was super sweet and fun, but that interacting with her beyond a friendly wave in passing would lead to nothing. Since I'd be moving to

England one of these years and she wouldn't understand my way of life, in my pride, I didn't give her a passing thought. She showed me great love after I realized what The Message was. She invited me to her Bible Study, and because I couldn't drive, she gave me rides.

I felt like such an outsider, but I quickly saw the great love that she, her boyfriend, and the leaders of the Bible study had, and felt that they truly cared about my story. I felt their compassion as I questioned every scripture that was read. "But you could interpret this scripture such and such a way," I would say, "so, how can we trust it, what does it mean?" and the hardest part of all, "Is this even true? What if it's not?" I had to wrestle with some hard questions. If The Message wasn't true, was Christianity? Was there even a God? What did it mean for my life if there was? What did it mean if there wasn't?

When I left The Message, for me, the default thing to go towards would have been atheism or agnosticism. Like many others, I was burned by religion and the concept of God, having seen faith used as a way to manipulate people and create an unhealthy judgmental community. Not to mention all the money in tithes that the church misappropriated, power misused, and theologically weak people confused and abused. I wondered, why am I not an atheist or agnostic?

I've grown to appreciate the phrase, 'Don't throw the baby out with the bathwater.' People can take a beautiful thing (like religion), and it can become distorted, and twisted for less than righteous intent. That doesn't automatically make all religions bad, and most importantly, it doesn't make God bad. I knew that concept to some degree, so I wanted to keep an open mind and look at how my choice would affect my life and purpose.

A very simple philosophical argument resonated with me, that is Pascal's Wager. In layman's terms, you can make a bet that either there is a God or there isn't. If you bet there is a God, you try to serve Him, and if you're right, then whatever eternal reward there is outside of time, is yours. If you lose the bet, then you just die and dissolve into eternal nothingness, no big deal. Same thing if you win the bet that there is no God—you presumably just die and slip out of consciousness. If however, you lose that latter bet, then you have to answer for that, and it might not be good. You will likely face some kind of judgment or eternal punishment according to many religions. So, it would seem the better of the two bets is to bet there is a God.

That bet made sense to me, so I resolved in my mind to bet that there is a God and try to serve Him, It seemed like the safer bet. So, what next? Which God? Why did I choose Jesus? No doubt, a huge part of it was the community I instantly found.

Coincidences—if you could call it that—lined up for me to be well equipped as my foundations of beliefs crumbled around me. I had two different philosophy classes around that time, and part of that was the apologetics Bible Study that Jenni took me to—where we learned about the evidence for the gospel. I wasn't only thinking about the evidence of the gospel and what I should believe, but how I wanted those beliefs to dictate what I did, or the way I portrayed myself. Naturally, one of the first behavior things that I questioned was the dress code I'd followed all my life.

My mother said she couldn't say anything against me wearing jeans from a biblical standpoint. "I feel a strong conviction about it," she'd say, and it reminded her of how she had grown up as Catholic, and one of her more pointed memories was seeing the women with very short dresses kneeling for prayer and revealing all. She also explained how she thought pants made women look like boys. So, I was bound to bound to obey my father and mother, but I stretched the rules here and there, perhaps because I'm a rebel. My rebellion included wearing the required uniform of black pants and a black T-shirt to the pizza buffet I worked at. I also started buying makeup and trying out subtle makeup looks, and eventually, I tried a red lip, positively shocking, I know.

I'd spent my whole life standing out and wearing things that were different from everyone else.

I knew I could handle myself, and that when people got to know the awkward girl that was Charity, they would like me for me; or at least, that's what I told myself. Something that really bugged me was when people would ask the reason I wore the skirts. I would have to say that it was my parent's religion, and since I lived in their house, I wanted to respect them. That would be true, but it made me look like a religious, legalistic, person. It made me look unapproachable, and I wanted people to approach me.

Well, if people wouldn't approach me, I'd have to come to them. I remember the fall of 2014 is when I met my dear friend, Autumn. She was a homeschooled girl like me, and we ended up sitting next to each other in math class. It occurred to me one day that I could try to be her friend. I would avoid people who wore jeans and earrings and cool bobbed haircuts, but I realized I was now allowed, by my permission, to make friends at school. One day when I arrived early for class, I saw her sitting out in the hallway, and I sat next to her,

"It was Autumn, right?" She looked up eagerly,

"Yes, and you were Charity, right?" We sat together, and I asked her about her life, and she asked about mine. I tried to ease in slowly and not let her see at first how bizarre my life was. It turns out, she was weird too, in her own quirky ways; and a friendship was born.

I took summer classes the last summer I was in Pennsylvania, and I participated in a swimming class. I'd never learned how to swim because I couldn't wear a swimsuit. I bought an expensive Message-approved swimming outfit, which was extremely cumbersome; a modest skirt with leggings, bra, and shirt which were all made from swim material. I also bought a modest one piece. It was tough to learn how to swim properly in the awkward modest outfit, but I wore it most of the time so that I could tell my parents I was wearing it. I didn't want to cause a fight over me wanting to wear a swimsuit. Sometimes, I wore the one piece instead. It was a minor argument, and it didn't cause me much grief to wear the unusual uniform—apart from embarrassment, which I was accustomed to at this point.

I had a boyfriend that summer too, from the church I'd started attending with Jenni (the girl from the apologetics Bible study), and we followed most of the rules my parents had given me. I didn't have the energy to fight rules like having a chaperone or not kissing. I was more focused on my education, trying to figure out my career goals, who I was, and what my faith was. After an eight month courtship without so much as holding hands, we broke up, on very good terms. I didn't know what my life held for me next, but I felt that there was something exciting on the horizon. I also felt very out of place in the four-year university I'd just transferred to, and I wondered if I even wanted to finish my degree in Pennsylvania, or if I wanted to finish my degree at all? Just as I was figuring out how to forgo my next semester, my brother, John (who was also out of The Message), offered me an internship position in D.C. working for a startup.

10

Moving to the Big City

No temptation has overtaken you that is not common to man.
God is faithful, and he will not let you be tempted beyond your
ability, but with the temptation he will also provide the way of
escape, that you may be able to endure it.

1 Corinthians 10:13 (ESV)

A job working for a startup in Washington, D.C. felt like a dream come true. I'd be lying if I said I wasn't sad to say goodbye to my friends and family in Pennsylvania, but this felt like what I'd been always waiting for, true freedom. I'd be living with a brother and one of our mutual friends. My new roommates would have similar values, but what I looked forward to the most; they couldn't control me. The first couple of months I lived in a closet of a room—that once a bed was in it, the floor space barely would have been enough to lay down

a yoga mat, but it was my space, my tiny, claustrophobic space.
Soon enough, however, my brother bought a little condo, and I
had a normal-sized room. I felt like I was living the dream.

Freedom at last, or was it? I didn't have the least idea what I
was doing. I found a church very quickly, one that my brothers
in D.C. had frequented. I also loved to swing dance, and I still
do. I'd only been out dancing a few times before, but never in
the big city. I went dancing almost every week, sometimes
more than once. I loved the 50's fashion and the swinging
tunes, and jazz which was once forbidden. I was ecstatic every
time I danced around the ballroom in a classy dress and
watched all the other dancers. I tied my hair in a swirly updo,
used a little gel to hold some waves, added a hair flower and
some pearls, and I danced most dances every night I was there;
I was a regular and almost an icon. The boys all knew me, and
although I rarely said yes to taking their numbers or going to
dinner, I sometimes did.

It was hard not to give some a chance, especially when some had a good reputation and were skilled dancers.

Although I went on dates with a handful of people in D.C., I never went on more than three dates with the same man. I had a long list of dating standards and character traits I was looking for in a potential significant other; and so often, the men I dated fell short. I was looking for a man of high integrity and wisdom, with a lot of charisma as well. There were a couple who may have met my standards, but they were too old, or I just didn't give them a chance.

In May, when I'd been in D.C. for almost a year, while at the dance halls I frequented so regularly, I met someone that I thought could be my Prince Charming. I thought to myself that he was the type of man I could fall in love with if I let myself.

I wrote a blog post about that lesson, and never posted it on my blog because I thought it was too raw, but here it is for you now:

"If you heard me mention recently that I was going through a rough spell, well, that's what this post is about. I'm about to get super vulnerable. One thing I'd like my blog to be is honest. I'm a very proud person in general, I'll admit that, but the last thing I want to do is come across as pretentious. Especially if I'm just sharing lessons learned ages ago, and acting as though I really have all the answers now. If I'm honest, sometimes, I feel like that. That mindset has helped me feel secure in my beliefs and confident because I strive not to be a hypocrite, and if I say I'm gonna do something, I'll strive to get it done. If I say I believe something, I'll live by it, end of story. Well, most of the time that's the end of the story.

About a month ago, I fell into a weird place. Essentially, I started questioning almost everything—my faith, family, friends, relationship status, goals, life's meaning, and my purpose. Did I say almost everything? I meant everything. The last time I felt like that was four years ago when I left The Message, and that time sparked a huge change in my life. I was worried and confused—what was on the other side this time?

I'm sure you have also experienced a time of questioning that intense as well? It seems to be a part of being human.

I feel like this could be a super helpful post for anyone who is going through this, or will, and I selfishly want to leave out all the details and just be all vague...but then this post would be all fluff, and just keep up my image. As much as I really want to do that, I also want to be honest, and super real about this lapse, so I'll tell you what I learned from it.

I'm not sure how it set on, it was a few things here and there, and then WHAM, I was full on in this state of depression, anxiety, and doubt of everything for some weeks. A big part (doubting Christianity), starts with how I have felt (for a while) that I don't really relate to a lot of Christians. I believe in Christianity, but I super respect other religions. Not to mention how many Christian doctrines and traditions I don't appreciate at all anymore. Thinking about it, I realized I could play devil's advocate really well if I wanted to talk someone out of Christianity. Even though I believe in it myself, I have a good grasp on debating and picking apart other people's arguments. I'm not the best, but I could even (I flatter myself) disprove my own arguments. Um…What? That realization is what left me so confused and a little depressed. It's very confusing to think you know it all when you don't know very much.

In talking with people of other religions, I realized a lot of my beliefs are a bit agnostic. No way of really knowing this or that until after death, when presumably we will get to ask all the questions, or we will simply fade out of existence entirely and then it won't matter either way.

Conveniently, I ran into an agnostic gentleman that was…well, pretty much everything on my formidable list of what I wanted in a guy, except he wasn't a Christian. What's the expression? *Stuff* hits the fan? I don't usually use profanity, so I'd like to keep the language on this blog PG. Things went south, the bottom dropped out, gone to hell in a handbasket, rubber hits the road, off the rails…You get what I'm saying, my state of mind could start having real implications in my life, *Stuff* got real.

I have a rule; I won't even go on one date with a guy if I already know something about him that doesn't meet my list. (Yeah, I know I sound so dehumanizing talking about a list...but it is something really important to me, and you can read about it in my post, 'The Dating Game'). And I don't go on a second date if I find something else. Likewise, not a third. I've kept to that rule pretty well, no matter how charming or how cool, if I knew something was a deal breaker, that'd be it. Hence, why I don't go on *too many* dates, and it kept me intentional with my goals.

So, he asked me on a date. At this point, I didn't know what his beliefs were, but he seemed like a *really nice guy, and I really liked him*. So, hoping he was a Christian, I was eager to go on a date with him. The date came and went, I hadn't broken any of my standards, right? However, I also completely avoided asking what his beliefs were on that date. I'm usually super intentional about dates, especially the first few. I always have fun, but there are things I want to know about a guy, so I don't waste either of our time. Well, he asked me on a second date. I said yes.

I was questioning everything, and this guy really did show up at the opportune time, when my opinions were in a rare place of pliability. Talk about a trial, everything else I could see about this guy was just green lights all the way, but I waited until close to the end of the second date to ask him about his faith. He already knew I was a Christian; it is not exactly something I can hide very well, nor did I try. I'll credit myself with that. He told me he was agnostic, explained what he believed. He was so competent, so respectful; it sounded really well thought out, I can't say the same for a lot of Christian guys. Instead of feeling that sinking feeling I had expected should his answer be anything but Christianity, I felt impressed. He was open-minded, intelligent, and could think for himself, I really related to that.

Where did I go wrong? If not, when I avoided the topic, then when I said yes to the third date. One of my guidelines is not to change any PREVIOUS guidelines or items on my list in the midst of being courted. It is one thing to really respect someone else's viewpoint, another to date someone with something so starkly different as that. Trouble is, one of the questions I had been pondering the weeks prior, was if I *really* needed to marry a Christian? So, when it turned out he wasn't, I felt stuck in limbo, uncertain.

Don't let your emotions make decisions for you. I tried to remind myself that, but it was really hard. It's easy enough to follow your standards if you never feel tempted to break them. I'd been tempted before to break those standards, but I'd always measured what would be the best outcome, and usually concluded that I should keep with those standards. This time though, I wasn't sure, what if all the stuff I thought was important didn't matter? What if I'd just built up this idealistic life and that was keeping me from truly falling in love? What if my standards were *gasp* too much?

Part of it was probably a cognitive dissonance thing since I was going on a date that didn't match up with my regular personal rules and beliefs. I started justifying and making excuses and finding all the reasons it was okay, or even better than my usual guidelines.

There is another standard I have, one I have many reasons for, which is that I don't want to have sex before marriage. It is one of those things that I knew even if my faith in Christianity fell apart, I'd keep. I've done my own research for it, so my reasons went beyond 'the Bible says so' or 'I think it is the way God intended it.' If you didn't know that about me...SURPRISE. Anyway, I knew I wanted to keep that; I was hoping he'd just say he had an issue with it, and then I would know it wasn't meant to be. I looked into some stats, and apparently, it's only like 3% of the population that actually have such standard (or stick with it anyway); So I figured the chances of him being fine with it were pretty slim. If he said he wasn't okay with it, then I wouldn't have to decide if the fact that he wasn't a Christian was an issue or not, I could take the easy way out with a different deal breaker.

The third date was coming to an end, and I had avoided bringing it up. It was nearing the end when I finally just started spitting it out, "There's a really awkward topic I've been avoiding bringing up." I knew once I said that, I wouldn't be able to back down and veer off topic. Normally, I don't have much trouble bringing up awkward topics, but part of me really wanted it to work with this guy. So, I told him and was prepared for his surprise and confusion. Yet, he didn't even flinch, and he was incredibly respectful, different from some 'Christian' guys I'd communicated that same standard to. He said he completely understood where I was coming from, and he said it wasn't all too uncommon in the place he'd lived prior. He said he respected it, that it wasn't as big of a deal as it seemed. He said he would be fine with it moving forward. He then added, honestly, that it wasn't something he'd upheld; it wasn't one of his standards, though he respected where I was coming from.

The intellectual side of my brain was like 'Hell no! Come on, react differently, this is too hard to decide! And you could just be faking it for now!' The other side of me...The more emotional, romantic side... 'Wow...He's so respectful, so nice; he's okay with it! You heard him! He really is a nice guy!'

"But you probably want someone who shares those same values...?" he asked with a bit of hesitation, even he saw the importance of it.

That question was the key that snapped me out of my stupor, "Yeah, I guess I do." Yeah, it's going to be hard to find someone who shares all my standards and skepticism too and all the other things that are vital to me, but I will continue to hold to it. Even if he was okay with that part, the whole dating a Christian thing was still crucial for me.

My takeaway from this experience has been a reminder to look at the big picture. I can see how much Christianity has benefitted me overall, if not for it to fall back on, I'd have a lot of regrets and emotional baggage to carry around. I'm a free spirit, and if not for the straight and narrow delayed gratification the Bible teaches, and what my parents taught me, I don't know where I'd be. I want my kids to grow up with those same values; I have a lot of vastly different viewpoints than my parents, but they instilled in me morals, standards, self-discipline, a curiosity to seek the truth, to work hard, etc., and I want to pass that on. I know you can have all that without religion, but it's a solid grounding, especially when you're young, and it's hard to see the big picture.

On the other side of that, I've started reading more again, praying more, and just trying to refocus. Also, eating that slice of humble pie has given me a little more empathy, more compassion for people who are really wrestling with right and wrong. Sure, it might not seem like the biggest deal, but for me, it was, I knew I'd be acting more on emotion than on objectivity. I knew I'd be compromising what I wanted for my life in the future because it seemed right in the moment. If you lose respect for yourself and your values, everything goes. If you think something is important, you should honor that. If you know you should be doing something, then do it. If you know you need to stop doing something, stop! If your moral compass is pulling you right, and you go left, you better turn right back around. You fall, you get back up.

Yes, do examine your beliefs and be ready to change, but check whether that change is based on emotions, or if it is a well-thought-out plan that will benefit you and those around you. Is that change honoring God? Change can be an amazing tool God uses in our lives to shape our character. When I left The Message, and I was questioning everything, I changed a lot. I had to reshape my whole foundation of beliefs. This time, the foundation was the same, but there were disciplines and heart attitude that I needed to focus on. I'm praying more, something I really didn't expect to ever be interested in. I don't really know all the ways my heart needs to change, but prayer and scripture seem like a good way to start.

The most important things in times like this involve seeking guidance and looking to the future. Don't do something that the futuristic you, ten years from now, will likely regret. As for my struggle with my faith, I've remembered what kept me from falling four years ago, (Pascal's Wager) that really believing there is a God, and doing your best to serve Him, will come in handy should we die and some form of heaven and hell should exist. Not to mention, the quality of life. If you believe something, and you stick by it, instead of just going wherever the wind blows, then you will be able to respect yourself, and that's incredibly important."

I share that exclusive blog post with you to show who I was as I was shifting. I have been a very proud person throughout my life as you may have seen from my tales. In D.C., I made a small salary, but I had a high taste which got me in a little credit card debt, and even though it felt like everyone wanted to be my friend, I ended up having very few. My pride left me keeping people at arm's length. I wanted everyone to see me not as a girl who was in a cult before, but as a classy lady. They may have seen that, but what they didn't see was my heart. I rarely showed my true self because I was scared if people saw the real me; they would run the other direction.

That experience back in D.C. opened up my heart to trusting God again. I was still trusting so much in my own abilities. The things my heart loved were not the things God loved. I had a long way to go—I still do, but I began to dissociate the God I was learning about in the scriptures and through prayer, with the mirage of God I was taught as a child. I began to love again. I found that it wasn't about Pascal's wager or quality of life, it was about who God was, and what He'd done for me. I began to let my pride fall, and pray reluctantly at first, then with more and more longing, "More of you Jesus, less of me."

11

More of You Jesus

Count it all joy, my brothers, when you meet trials of various kinds, for you know that the testing of your faith produces steadfastness.

James 1:2-3 (ESV)

That mini heartbreak (which wasn't a true heartbreak), opened up my eyes. I didn't just want my faith to be some kind of ticket to heaven. I wanted to actually serve the God who had saved my life. I felt similar to the way I felt when I stopped believing in the cult back in 2014; it was death to my old self and old way of life. I wanted to really believe, not just with my head, but with my heart, in a God who would save my soul. I'd never experienced a God who would love me unconditionally like that, and it was hard to serve Him with a hardened heart. I didn't particularly want to read daily scriptures or pray, but I wanted to serve God; I wanted to make Him the center of my life for real.

So, I thought one of the ways to do that was to actually take time to serve Him and to get to know His heart through the reading of the scriptures, and for Him to get to know my heart through prayer. I began to realize however, that prayer was actually more about God changing my heart, growing me closer to Him. I didn't realize it when I started, but I believe He knew my heart already. Days turned to weeks and the few scriptures I read every morning turned into a chapter. Since when had I dubbed the Bible unnecessary? There was so much power and wisdom packed into its pages. If I read self-help books, how much more could I make time for a book about how God helps us? How He loves and cares for us? How we can love and serve Him?

My heart was shifting more and more. I started to feel content, but restless at the same time (if such a feeling is possible). I felt that I wasn't where I should be.

Where should I be then? What should I be doing? I felt that I needed to move, move somewhere and work on the gifts God had given me to serve Him. I opened up my heart to the possibility that D.C. wasn't where I should stay, but where? I did extensive research perchance God really was calling me somewhere else. I cross-referenced cultures, demographics, weather, markets, and other factors that I thought I wanted; Finally, I came to Austin, Texas. There were a few others on the list, but Austin kept showing up in some way or another—outshining the others.

I knew there would be no one I knew there. Would I be moving across the country all alone? That seemed a bit radical. How would I even be able to find roommates? Well, I thought, if I had to move there, how would I go about it? So, I looked up some churches in the Austin area, read through some mission statements, and I finally emailed about five churches asking if they knew how I could find a roommate or roommates of upstanding character. One of them, the Austin

Stone, got back to me, so I investigated roommates who went to that church.

Before I knew it, I found an awesome low-cost opportunity. I was excited, and the girl who was moving out seemed eager for me to have the place, but she said that a friend of hers was coming to look at the place first. I prayed that if it were God's will, I'd get the place or another location at a similar price point. I knew though that the other girl who was there in person was more likely to get it, and how did I know she wasn't praying too?

Finally, the girl who was moving out told me her friend did want the place, I sighed many sighs and went back to searching. Then the first girl called me back, "Another girl is moving out of our apartment and my friend is going to take that room, so mine is open again, do you want it?" I did a little happy dance; I had really wanted it. I knew in the excitement of that moment how much I wanted this thing. My one reservation was they needed someone ASAP. Was I ready to move? John prompted me, "If you're going to move, why wait?" So I dove in, I paid the first month's rent and started packing up my belongings, the place was mine in a couple of weeks.

I planned to buy a car and drive down, but I heard that I could get around without a car there, and could ride a bike or Uber to get to where I needed to go, (word to the wise, moving to a new city without a car is risky business). So, I thought I'd rent a moving truck or go with a friend who was old enough to rent one and then pay for their flight back. My parents jumped in and offered to drive me down. I had just sprained my ankle and driving a great distance using that foot on the pedal was not appealing to me. After thinking about their offer, I gladly accepted their help.

So, that's how I ended up here in Austin, Texas in July of 2018, with zero friends apart from Jesus. My parents helped me unpack, and then they headed back. When they left, it was just me. I'd met one of my roommates for a moment, and hers was the only name I knew in Texas. I cried a few tears; I won't lie. Normally, when I'm sad and anxious, I'm not exactly in the mood to be social with new people (I'd rather it be trusted close friends in such cases), but in this case, the reason I was sad and anxious was that I didn't have any friends. So, I felt I had no choice; I would just have to stop the tear flow long enough to have conversations with people. I looked up the church I wanted to go to and found their various locations and service times. I'd go to a couple of those at one or two campuses. I looked up events around Austin. I'd go to those, and I got a dating app and a friend-finding app. I'd try to fill up my days as much as I could with social things. I had to, I was a social person fueled by being around people I cared about and who cared about me, but there was no one like that in Texas yet.

So, I went on some dates, with men looking for love and coffee dates with girls who were looking for friends. I Ubered to church and cried through all the songs. I tried to look normal, and not be an emotional wreck, but the truth is, I was mourning. Mourning my popularity and comfort of my home in D.C.

Fast forward a month, and my dive head first approach had got me very well connected. Even though my friendships were all new, I started to settle in because I knew the trajectory of those friendships was good. I was being very vulnerable with those friends. I was starting to feel at home. If nothing else though, being in Austin with no friends, moving on a whim, or led by the Spirit or whatever you want to call it—it taught me the true frailty of my nature. I saw that I wasn't truly self-sufficient. I needed other people, and I especially needed my Savior.

Since I moved to Austin, or more notably, since that fateful meeting with the agnostic prince charming several months before that, the trajectory of my life changed. I couldn't have foreseen it; I didn't really know what I was getting into. I had big dreams I wanted to pursue for my own glory, and God just swept in and changed my heart. Unexpectedly, money or status didn't matter. Suddenly, there was a constant question on my heart, "How can I show Jesus to people?" He is amazing, and I want people to know. For instance, I've always wanted to

177

be an author, but to share the story of how I left The Message? That seemed like something way too vulnerable to share with the world. It seemed way too controversial, and I didn't feel that being in a cult painted me in a good light. That's just it though; this story isn't really about me. It's not about the way I lived my life, or how I escaped a cult, or how I changed my life. It's about God's grace and mercy for me. The desire for me to keep up some kind of acceptable image for myself is overshadowed by how much God has done for me that I couldn't have done for myself. If it were left up to me to write my story, it would have way fewer bumps and a lot more pride. As it is, I want you to know how broken I am and how healing God is. So you see, this story is all for glory, not my glory, but God's. I couldn't have known five years ago where life would take me, but I'm very glad someone knew then where I'd be now, and knows now where I'll be another five years from now.

One of my dear friends from Austin told me an angle to the story of Joseph that'd I'd like to share with you. If you don't know the story, it is found at the end of Genesis. Joseph is the favorite of his father, and since his brothers are so jealous, they sell him into slavery in Egypt. Joseph suffers much, spending jail time for wrong accusations, being forgotten, and eventually, he serves the pharaoh—soon, the Pharoah makes him his right-hand man. Later, his brothers see him again and plead for forgiveness. There is much more to that story, but something that my friend pointed out to me was the words he said to his brothers: "As for you, you meant evil against me, but God meant it for good, to bring it about that many people should be kept alive, as they are today" (Genesis 50:20).

I knew this verse before, but what I didn't realize were the words used in the initial text. The word there, 'meant,' when referring to the brothers' intent is a Hebrew word for weaving, like weaving a tapestry. The next time though, where it is used for God's intent, the word, 'meant' is a different word for 'weaving,' a weaving like a grandmaster would weave. I must remind myself of this. The things in my life that seem so

179

hard, God was working out for good, weaving a *master* tapestry that no amount of planning on my part could begin to fathom.

I'm learning how to pray. When I was a child, I prayed for a man I never knew; that he would be healed. I was taught and believed that if you just had enough faith in prayer, that God would answer it. *If you just had enough faith.* At times, I had so much faith that when Brother Coleman wasn't healed, I was legitimately shocked. I had faith like the way you believe a chair is behind you when you go to sit down. The truth is, sometimes, God says no; sometimes His ways aren't our ways, and that's good because He has a masterplan. It will work out for His glory. I'm learning to have faith, that God will answer my prayers in the way that is best for me.

Romans 8:28 says that He works all things together for good for those who love God. That's where my faith lies. I'm learning to pray that way, and I know God hears my prayers and sees my tears. Even when I don't understand why things happen, I know He is a good Father.

My prayer for this book is that God would intercede in the hearts of those who read this. That He would expose the lies in our heart that as infants, we heard, and when we could understand, we clung to. I pray that He would open your eyes daily as He has done and continues to do for me.

My story may seem bizarre, but in many ways, it's not at all. You and I are not that different. I grew up in a broken environment that I slowly realized wasn't ideal. I learned to accept it and call that my reality. Those broken parts of your story? Those pieces cannot be changed, but you haven't seen all the ways those pieces play out in the rest of your story. Your story doesn't end at your past. I pray that you would experience the love and grace of Jesus Christ, where once we were dead in sin, He breathes into us a new life.

12

Truth that Sets me Free

So Jesus said to the Jews who had believed him, "If you abide in my word, you are truly my disciples, and you will know the truth, and the truth will set you free."

John 8:31-22 (ESV)

Since I still have your attention, there is one more thing I need to do before closing out my experience. I'd like to illustrate what I was taught—both explicitly and implicitly in my upbringing in The Message, and what I've learned since then. Keep in mind; I'm still learning. It feels like it has been such a long journey to learn what the Gospel of Jesus Christ is really all about, but I am still very young. Bits and pieces of doctrine where the Bible has been misappropriated still cling to my subconscious. I'm sure if I were writing this same book in five or ten years from now, I'd have a better grasp of the Truth. I'd like to share points; however, that show you what I mean when I say that Jesus did rescue me. I want to show you His grace, just in case it isn't plain for you in my narrative thus far. Please, indulge me as I tell you about a few specific spiritual disciplines and doctrines. I want you to see what He has done in my heart and mind so that you too can recognize fallacies you've believed about God.

One of the things that helped me grow the most this past year has been prayer. It has sparked so much healing in my heart, and new patterns of thinking and habits have sprung from those heart changes. So, it seems fitting that I contrast how I understand prayer now, compared to when I was in The Message and what I've learned since leaving. In the topic of prayer, I was taught that God had the power to move mountains and that if I had the faith of a mustard seed and prayed, God would answer my prayer in the way I believed.

You've seen this encapsulated in my prayers for Brother Coleman. I believed so hard that God would heal him! As I've articulated already, I believed with so much faith that I was surprised when he wasn't healed. God didn't heal him though; so, what does that mean? And if I didn't have enough faith, surely there was someone else in the church who had, if it were possible, more faith than me. So, why wasn't he healed? Because that is not a biblical view of prayer or God. God is not a light switch we can turn on and off to get our way in the trials of this life. In telling us how to pray (Matthew 6:5-15), Jesus first tells us how *not* to pray. He says we should not make a show of our prayers like the Pharisees and think not that because of our many words, we will be heard. In other words, your prayers are between you and God, and technique in prayer won't get your prayers answered. *"Oh, but if you just have enough faith!"*

Yes, have faith in God's power to answer your prayer but also have faith that God will work all things together for good for those who love God (Romans 8:28). Jesus tells us to pray with reverence and familiarity:

(a) 'Our Father' means we have **a personal relationship** with Him.

(b) 'Who's in Heaven, Hallowed be your name' shows despite our relationship with Him, **He's holy, to be revered, all-powerful**. Jesus teaches us to pray for our needs;

(c) 'Give us this day our daily bread.' **We pray for our most basic needs**.

(d)He also teaches us to repent of our sin and **extend the grace and mercy we experience from God, to others**, 'and forgive us our trespasses, as we forgive those who trespass against us.'

(e) He also teaches us to pray, 'Your will be done, on earth as it is in heaven.' That's what I wanted to get to. **We should pray for God's will in our life**, not our own. Sure, I knew this passage of scripture like you might know the face of an acquaintance, but I didn't really know it.

I heard a sermon at my local church on this topic a few weeks into editing this book. The pastor spent a moment to touch on how some extremist religious groups use this lie about prayer (That if you have enough faith, God will answer you the way you want) to manipulate and control, to give weak people false hope and power. What does this teach us about God and ourselves when that thing we prayed for doesn't come to fruition?

I was sobbing during that service. I knew I must have looked like an idiot as the pastor moved passed that point, and my tears weren't done falling. That was how I had been taught prayer all my life, and I only got a better grasp on it this past year, since the teaching of my youth had lingered on. That may have been what started my tears, but the thing that kept the waterworks flowing long after the pastor had moved on was something else. I was suddenly keenly aware that there are people out there right now, who believe those crushing lies with their whole heart—there are people in The Message and other religious groups preaching that false doctrine right now.

"God," I mouthed a prayer in the church. "God, why? It's not right; it's not just. They are trying to know you in prayer, but they do not know your true nature. They are hurting and coming to you, and then they wonder why you don't hear them! They are being led by doctrines that teach them that if they have enough faith, you will hear, and do as they ask. Please, expose that lie; show them that you are with them and for them even when things don't happen the way they pray! Someone needs to tell them that!"

I've not just learned that God hears me when I pray, but that prayer is a gift from God to shift our hearts more towards Him and His will. I've learned that He works things together for good in the long run. I've learned that the way we should pray is the way Jesus did in Gethsemane when He knows the suffering which is about to happen to Him, "My Father, if it is possible, let this cup pass from Me; nevertheless, let it be as You, not I, would have it." Then, a little while later, He said, "If this cup cannot pass by, but I must drink it, Your will be done!" He does pray and ask His father if there is any other way, but He also surrenders His will to the Father.

One of the things that prayer prompted me to do was to read more scripture. I wanted to know God's heart. I'd read the Bible cover to cover while I was a preteen/teenager in The Message. I thought I 'knew' its contents. James 1:22-24 (ESV) talks about knowing the Word and doing it,

But be doers of the word, and not hearers only, deceiving yourselves. For if anyone is a hearer of the word and not a doer, he is like a man who looks intently at his natural face in a mirror. For he looks at himself and goes away and at once forgets what he was like. But the one who looks into the perfect law, the law of liberty, and perseveres, being no hearer who forgets but a doer who acts, he will be blessed in his doing.

This is something I thought I did. I followed a lot of *rules*, but I started realizing that even after I'd left The Message, a certain thought pattern remained. I was picking and choosing what I wanted to act on in the scripture after I left The Message, the same way The Message ministers had done. Instead of wrestling with the Word of God, looking at the general context, historical context, cross-referencing, and praying over hard passages of scripture, I would ignore them. I was a Pharisee. Please, do not quote me as someone who has all this figured out, because I'm still learning to take God at His Word.

Writing this book is one of those acts of obedience. I saw the depravity in The Message and wanted to reach out with the truth. I wanted to speak with boldness so that those who wanted to hear could hear me. I say that, but really, the thought of writing such a book was scary, saying I 'wanted' to write this book is a complicated statement. Being a published author has been a dream of mine for a long time, but I wanted to write a fictional tale, not a controversial memoir. However, I couldn't get it out of my head or my heart. If I really were putting God first in my life, I would have to give up some of my desire for approval and control. I'd have to surrender to

Him; I'd have to write this book to the best of my ability, and let Him use it as He sees fit.

To carry this out, I knew I'd need strength, I'm a young person, riddled with anxiety, pride, and idols of control and approval that often cloud my judgment. I couldn't have written this if not for daily strength found in the Word of God. Reading scripture almost every day gave me the strength to face my struggles. It has also given me the wisdom and fortitude I needed for this undertaking. The Word of the Lord challenges us. It is confrontational, convicting, humbling, and full of grace. Likewise, our God; He gives us the freedom to live life and choose our paths while giving us the tools we need and holding our hand along the way if we let Him.

I couldn't have written this book without help and support. Without fact checkers and wise counsel, I would be a fool to think, even with all of those steps I've taken, that this book would be without fault. I am acknowledging that now. I am not a perfect person, but through my imperfect act, I want God's character to shine through. That is my intent, but I know by writing this, I am being held to a higher standard because my words could impact more than just those close to me. That is why I wanted help; because to state something about God on a public scale is a big deal, which brings me to my next point. What about pastors?

James 3:1-2 (ESV) says, "Not many of you should become teachers, my brothers, for you know that we who teach will be judged with greater strictness. For we all stumble in many ways." Notice this passage doesn't say that some people will not stumble, and those should be pastors. No, it's saying that there is a greater standard for those who preach, even though they are humans too. If you have a lot of authority and people look to you for spiritual guidance, you should have more accountability, not less. You should pray over what you plan to say more, not less. You should read scripture more, not less. Those in a teaching position carry a lot of weight on their shoulders when they're serving well. I used the word 'serving' very intentionally because that is how Jesus taught His disciples to be leaders. I have great respect for those in ministry; it is hard to carry all that authority and have the responsibility to lead people well.

However, that's not what I was taught a pastor should be when I was growing up. Sometimes, a pastor would say something like, "We've graduated from the Bible, that is milk to us. The words of Brother Branham is the meat we need!" I'd bet my bottom dollar that someone who would say such a thing to their congregation was not having daily devotions themselves. I was taught too, implicitly and explicitly, that those in ministry were closer to (if not at) perfection than we were. The things they said from the pulpit were all perfect, and exactly what God wanted them to say.

I had to learn that it's okay to question things a pastor says; after all, he is a human, not God. It's okay to trust that the things he's preaching, he has researched with scripture and prayed about, but you'd be a fool if you took his sermon as scripture. It starts to become downright toxic if that is something you are explicitly told to do. A pastor should encourage his congregation to question his words and to wrestle with the scripture themselves. Christianity is about personal relationships with Christ—being a part of a church helps you with that, but it is by no means a substitute for individual study.

The Bible is a complex book. Recently, it has become my favorite. It teaches wisdom and tells a historical narrative. When reading the scripture, it is important to cross-reference, check the context of what is being said (by reading the surrounding chapters) and by knowing the historical and geographical context (what was the cultural and social issues at the time the scriptures were written?); perhaps even the linguistic nuances of the translation from Greek or Hebrew (Something I am yet to study). This is something that makes the Bible so inexhaustible. It's such a long narrative, and there are so many times, places, and cultures that build upon each other to tell the gospel story. If you are a Christian, you should apply the wisdom of the scripture to your life to the best of your ability. 2nd Timothy 3:16-17 (ESV) says, "All Scripture is breathed out by God and profitable for teaching, for reproof, for correction, and for training in righteousness, that the man of God may be complete, equipped for every good work."

The Bible itself teaches that you don't simply 'graduate' from the Bible. Contrary to what I was taught in The Message, there is no end to your study. It isn't something you can read once and never come back to. Hebrew 4:12 (ESV) says, "For the word of God is living and active, sharper than any two-edged sword, piercing to the division of soul and of spirit, of joints and of marrow, and discerning the thoughts and intentions of the heart."

The Bible says not to add or take away from it: "You shall not add to the word that I command you, nor take from it, that you may keep the commandments of the LORD your God that I command you" (Deuteronomy 4:2 ESV). This was quoted a lot in The Message by William Branham, Brother Coleman, and others who used it to say that you shouldn't abridge what they said (implying even when they weren't saying explicitly, that their words were equal to the scriptures). Brother Branham claimed he took the scriptures word for word in the King James Version Bible. Yet he also taught doctrines that added on to scripture; to name one, he taught the Serpent Seed doctrine, which I'll explain briefly. The Biblical narrative that this doctrine pulls from is the story in Genesis of how Adam and Eve are tempted by the serpent to eat of the forbidden fruit. Eve is the first to take a bite, and then Adam also eats from the tree. They are cast out of paradise, and they give birth to Cain and Abel. The serpent seed doctrine teaches that Eve actually had *sex* with the serpent, and Cain was the serpent's son, while Abel was the son of Adam[10]. If that's not adding to the Bible, I don't know what is.

Something crucial to the Christian faith is to share it. This is a discipline known as the Great Commission. Even though The Message claims to be 'nondenominational Christianity,' they sidestep Jesus's final request to His disciples: 'And Jesus came and said to them, "All authority in heaven and on earth has been given to me. Go therefore and make disciples of all nations, baptizing them in the name of the Father and of the Son and of the Holy Spirit, teaching them to observe all that I have commanded you. And behold, I am with you always, to the end of the age"' (Matthew 28:16-20; ESV). As Christians, we are called to share the gospel with people boldly. If The Message preached the gospel, they would be telling their congregations to share the good news instead of hiding it, but I'm sure you can tell by now, The Message is not founded on biblical truth, and that is not what they taught me.

The Message uses verses like Romans 12:2, "Do not be conformed to this world, but be transformed by the renewal of your mind, that by testing you may discern what is the will of God, what is good and acceptable and perfect" as justification for sheltering themselves from the world, but that's not what this verse is talking about. This verse and others like it teaches us not to wrap up our identity and purpose in things of this world as non-believers do because our identity is in Christ. We are free from vain pursuits of instant gratification and earthly pleasures because those things shouldn't be what define us. We are building up our treasures in heaven. Where we place our trust and faith in should be different than non-Christians, but we shouldn't be scared to hang out with a non-believer or share our faith. That is not the gospel. Jesus not only leaves us with guidelines of what our interactions with non-believers should be but also shows us by example. He is a friend to tax collectors, drunkards, idolaters, scribes, fishermen, and beggars. He was a light to them, speaking truth to them and quoting Old Testament scripture all the time. He knew the Scripture, and He shared it. He loved and served people. That is the Jesus I now know.

Yes, have a Christian community that will spur you on towards Christ; that is Biblical! That community shouldn't cut you off from non-Christians though; we are called to share with people who are not Christians. Hebrews 10:23-25 (ESV) says, "Let us hold fast the confession of our hope without wavering, for he who promised is faithful. And let us consider how to stir up one another to love and good works, not neglecting to meet together, as is the habit of some, but encouraging one another, and all the more as you see the Day drawing near." We should hold each other accountable and remind ourselves what the gospel is, encouraging one another to know God's heart through prayer and scripture, to be able to give an answer when someone asks about your faith and to share with others, that they might receive the gift of salvation. I want you to see the gospel in my story of redemption, but my story is only important because it shows how THE story of redemption, that is, the story of Jesus's death and resurrection, has impacted my life and brought me from death to life. Lest along my journey I confused that gospel at all, I want to lay it out for you simply in a few short paragraphs with many scriptural references, because I don't want you to take my word for it. This is the gospel:

We are all sinners, not worthy to enter Heaven, without any sin in our lives, in our past, present or future. "Or do you not know that the unrighteous will not inherit the kingdom of God?" (1 Corinthians 6:9; ESV), and "For you may be sure of this, that everyone who is sexually immoral or impure, or who is covetous (that is, an idolater), has no inheritance in the kingdom of Christ and God" (Ephesians 5:5; ESV). It is impossible for us to be without sin, we are humans and we sin every day. As much as we'd like to say that it is possible, we are constantly giving in to temptations. "If we say we have no sin, we deceive ourselves, and the truth is not in us. If we confess our sins, he is faithful and just to forgive us our sins and to cleanse us from all unrighteousness. If we say we have not sinned, we make him a liar, and his word is not in us" (1 John 1:8-10; ESV).

That is why God sent His Son to bear our sins on His shoulders, to bear the brunt of our sin, to pay the penalty for all the crimes ever to be committed, to this I can recount the verse that you have likely heard, even if you are not a Christian, "For God so loved the world, that he gave his only Son, that whoever believes in him should not perish but have eternal life" (John 3:16). That verse is so popular because it simplifies the gospel so beautifully to its core elements. God offers the free gift of eternal life to all who repent for their sins and call on His name (Yes, ALL), and those who will admit and repent of their ways, by also professing that they believe in who Jesus is and His promise; they will be counted sinless before the throne of God. Not Because of who we are or what we've done, but because of who He is and what He's done for us. John 1:13 (ESV) says, "But to all who did receive him, who believed in his name, he gave the right to become children of God."

"For the wages of sin is death, but the free gift of God is eternal life in Christ Jesus our Lord." (Romans 6:23; ESV) That gospel is what I believe when it is simply boiled down, and the fact of the matter is, it is that simple. Jesus died for our sins, and whoever repents and believes in Him has the gift of eternal life. Those words stir up a deep spring of joy and gratitude in me, which floods from my soul. The more I study, the clearer that simple truth is. The more I understand about the gospel and all the complexities I study, the more I realize that nothing I can do can earn this grace, and the more I genuinely desire to walk with integrity. Not for a moment did I think that I can earn my salvation but instead, earnestly fascinated by the disciplines described by a Man who would die for me, and by the Words of the book that tells of His story. I strive after righteousness because I'm in love with Jesus and what's close to His heart, I want it to be close to mine too.

Jesus is coming was long foretold, people were waiting for a Messiah to come, but they weren't expecting Jesus to be that One—the Son of God playing the part of a humble carpenter's son, who ate with the outcasts of society, healed the sick, and preached of love more than anything else. Many didn't see who He was at the time or now, even though one by one, He fulfilled all the Old Testament prophecies surrounding His birth, life, death, and resurrection. After leaving a cult, I chose the Lord Jesus for His evident historical backing and the way He lived His life on earth, but ultimately, being a Christian is a decision to serve a living God—repentance of your sin and asking your Savior to be the Lord of your life. Being a Christian is accepting His amazing grace and humbly walking in faith. It's not about your works, "For by grace you have been saved through faith. And this is not your own doing; it is the gift of God, not a result of works, so that no one may boast" (Ephesians 2:8-9).

Do you remember the Willow tree? The one that I played around as a child? The Willow tree whose branches we tugged on? The one whose branches we turned into crowns and bracelets? The Willow tree of my childhood? The willow tree that was 'base' for us when we played freeze tag? Well, if you drove past that little church in Pennsylvania, you won't find it. Around the time I left, I found out that it had died, and since it could not be brought back to life, it was cut down.

I thought I knew where I was going. My roots, they were in that church, that's where I grew, and that's where I thought I'd continue to grow. My supposed destiny was not set. Like that willow who died and was cut down, my time in that church came to an end with my childhood. I grew and learned from those circumstances, both good and bad. I had to find out what was true, and not just with my head but with my heart and actions. Yes, I have some roots there, but those old beliefs that bound me are dead. Christ has redeemed my story, I have found new life in Him. May all the glory be to Him.

Therefore, if anyone is in Christ, he is a new creation. The old has passed away; behold, the new has come.

2 Corinthians 5:17 (ESV)

Appendix

[1] (page 6) In regards to William Branham's birth, there are 3 archived documents that give different accounts of his birth, including a marriage license to his first wife Hope Brumbach on which he writes his birthday as April 8, 1908. Over seven years later (After the death of his first wife) he writes April 6, 1909 as his birthdate on his marriage certificate to Meda Broy. The closest thing to a birth certificate that is archived is a census report his parents filled out on April 15, 1910 stating that he was 3 years old, which would mean his birthday would have to be April 14, 1907 at the latest.
On September 29, 1961 Branham asserted that he was born on March 10, 1907 (William Branham, 51-0929 - Our Hope is in God, para. 8).
On the 19th of April 1959 he said he was born on April 6th, 1909 (William Branham, 59-0419A - My Life Story, para. 44).

[2] (page 6) The story of Branham's birth, according to Branham (William Branham, 52-0713A - Early Spiritual Experiences, para. 12).

[3] (page 7) William Branham claims he was commissioned in his ministry many times, here is one of the times he cited the Cloud to be part of that commission (William Branham, 65-1206 - Modern Events Are Made Clear by Prophecy, para. 320).

[4] (page 7) Estimated at between 500,000 and 1,000,000 people in 2019, ("Commission & Ministry." BelieveTheSign, 20 Apr. 2019, www.believethesign.com/index.php?title=Commission_&_Ministry.)

Online Resources

Although I have done much research on my own, I am very thankful (truly eternally thankful) for the team over at the Believe the Sign website. (www.BelievetheSign.com) for their detail-oriented research. They were once an advocate of the Message, but after they researched into some questions a sceptic asked, they turned around their website, admitting they were wrong for believing in The Message ("Humble Pie." BelieveTheSign, 14 Mar. 2013, en.believethesign.com/index.php/Humble_Pie.)

If you have more questions about The Message, they articulate points far better than I ever could, including intensive cross-referencing of scripture and William Branham's quotes. This book has been my testimony of leaving The Message, not a full account of why The Message is not credible. BelieveTheSign elaborates on The Message more extensively than I have room for here.

For searching William Branham quotes or looking up quotes that I've cited to see them in context, please use The Table by Voice of God Recordings, (www.Table.Branham.org) it is a site by and for Message believers.

If you have further questions about The Message, my experience in general, or if you would like to share your story with me, please send all correspondence to WhereTheWillowWeeps@gmail.com. I'd love to hear from you!

Although I may not be able to respond to each email, I will address repeated questions on my blog, which you can find at, www.ThisArtistsLife.com.

Thank you for letting me share my story with you, I pray that it was a blessing to you.